Powerful Profits from

SLOTS

ALSO BY THE AUTHOR

Casino Magazine's Play Smart and Win
(Simon & Schuster/Fireside, 1994)

Casino Games Made Easy
(Premier, 1999)

Powerful Profits from Blackjack
(Kensington, 2003)

*Casino GambleTalk: The Language of Gambling and
New Casino Games*
(Kensington, 2003)

Powerful Profits from Craps
(Kensington, 2003)

Powerful Profits from Video Poker
(Kensington, 2003)

Advanced Strategies for Casino Games
(Kensington, 2004)

Powerful Profits from Casino Keno
(Kensington, 2004)

Ultimate Internet Gambling
(Kensington, 2004)

Powerful Profits from

SLOTS

Victor H. Royer

Lyle Stuart
Kensington Publishing Corp.
www.kensingtonbooks.com

LYLE STUART BOOKS are published by

Kensington Publishing Corp.
850 Third Avenue
New York, NY 10022

All Kensington titles, imprints, and distributed lines are available at special quantity discounts for bulk purchases for sales promotions, premiums, fund-raising, educational, or institutional use. Special book excerpts or customized printings can also be created to fit specific needs. For details, write or phone the office of the Kensington special sales manager: Kensington Publishing Corp., 850 Third Avenue, New York, NY 10022, attn: Special Sales Department, phone 1-800-221-2647.

Lyle Stuart is a trademark of Kensington Publishing Corp.

First printing: March 2003

10   9   8   7   6   5   4   3

Printed in the United States of America

Library of Congress Control Number: 2002113509

ISBN 0-8184-0640-2

This book is gratefully dedicated to

Mr. Ed Rogich

for his foresight and vision

and to

Mr. Rick Sorensen

for his many years of friendship and assistance

"Veni, vidi, vici"—I came, I saw, I conquered.
—Julius Caesar

Remember this each time you go to a casino.

Contents

Foreword

In the world of gambling, slot machines are a recent phenomenon. In fact, they can easily be called the "baby" of the gaming revolution. What we now know as the slot machine is barely over one hundred years old. Even though there were several mechanical gambling machines prior to 1895, it was not until Charles Fey made the classic three-reel Liberty Bell slot machine in San Francisco in 1895 that the true modern era of the slot machine began.

Other forms of gambling have been around for centuries. Throughout recorded history, mankind's past is rich in gambling. Some six thousand years ago, the early Egyptians used dice made from bone. Some of these artifacts have been recovered from archeological sites in Egypt and the lower Nile valley. As old as some of the dice are, they look remarkably similar to the dice we use today in the game of craps. Other civilizations invented their own forms of gambling. Some four thousand years or so ago, the Chinese invented playing cards and began to shuffle these in ways that later became the kind of casino-style playing cards we now use.

But the slot machine had to wait for the nineteenth-century Industrial Revolution, a time when the world began to see the viability of machines, first in industrial and farm use, then in factories, then in locomotion and transport, and finally in gambling. The slot machines that resulted from Charles Fey's invention became the standard model. All slot machines in use today owe their appearance, and their heritage, to those early mechanical clunkers.

Early slot machines used iron reels, lead weights, and gears and stoppers to achieve the desired results. They were spring-loaded, and inserting the coin (yes, most of these machines took only *one* coin back then) freed the handle so that the player was able to pull the lever on the side of the machine. This released the reels, which then began to spin until their stoppers caught them and stopped them. This happened in turn, from left to right, and was accompanied by loud clanking noises, hence the expression "old clunkers." The winning combinations were determined by the number of stops along each of the reels. Pulling the handle was hard, and these machines were highly prone to manipulation and misuse. Cheating was easy, by the use of slugs instead of coins, by the use of misaligned or fraudulently weighted weights on the reels, by handle-pulls, by slamming, and by a variety of other methods and cheating techniques. These early machines were notoriously bad payers, and that's how they got their nickname "the one-armed bandit."

For more than eighty years, slot machines were virtually stagnant in development. Little changed in the way they looked or the way they were made. Meanwhile, the world changed around them. The modern era began after the end of World War II, and still the slot machine was much the same as it was back in 1899. Casinos viewed the slot machine as a necessary evil. Very little revenue came from them. No wonder, since most of these machines still took only one coin at a time and the jackpots were very limited. Then in the 1960s, a new innovation came forward. This was the invention of the coin hopper, a device that could pay out multiple coins. Up until that time, the machine itself not only had to hold the entire jackpot, but it could pay out only a certain amount for other, smaller, non-jackpot pays. Significant varieties of pays were simply impossible, and the number of reels and stops was limited. With the addition of the coin hopper, the machine could now pay out many more winning combinations, and this also allowed for many more stops on the reels.

As good as this innovation was, the slot machine was still looked upon by the casino industry as a mere diversion. All the really heavy gambling was done on table games. More than 80 percent of the casinos' revenues came from gamblers playing table games. The slots were there primarily so that the women—the wives and girlfriends of the "real" gamblers—would have something to do while the men gambled on the real games. Casinos tolerated slot machines because of this, and never really considered them a real source of revenue. But then, as with life, it all changed.

In the early 1970s, the microprocessor became commercially available. Still a decade away from being used in personal computers, and in just about everything we now take for granted, this innovation would have far-reaching consequences for the slot machines. By the 1980s, computers began to filter into the mainstream of society, as people began to buy home computers. The availability of computer technology spurred the development of numerous modern marvels, one of which was the modern slot machine. What we now see in the casinos as the slot machine really began life in the computer era. Even though these machines may look like the old mechanical reel machines, they are not. All the slot machines now on the casino floor are controlled by computers, no matter what they may look like. Initially, the slot machines were still made to look, feel, and sound like the old mechanical ones. These were called "electromechanical" slot machines and were a kind of intermediate step between the purely mechanical and the purely electronic, or computerized, slot machine. The introduction of the electromechanical slot machines was done largely to keep the players from thinking the new machines were somehow "rigged." Most of the players at that time had a familiarity with the mechanical kinds of slots, and the "feel" of the electromechanical slot machines made these players more comfortable at the new games. This feel and look of the machines was in reality a mere illusion, because even the electromechanical slots no longer operated on reels with reel-stoppers, as the old machines used to. This mindset kept the video slots from reaching the mainstream casinos for more than a decade after the invention of computer processors powerful enough to be able to run them. People weren't ready for video slots, and at that time—back in the 1980s—many people still weren't ready for the computerized reel slots. They still wanted the old mechanical feel, and so that's what they got. Even today, many reel slot machines are still made to look like—and in some case also feel like—the old clunkers.

Advances in computer technology allowed for the proliferation of slot machines at a staggering rate. Suddenly, jackpots in the tens of thousands of dollars were possible. Even jackpots in the hundreds of thousands and millions of dollars could now be programmed, because the computer could store the necessary information to allow for the multiple "virtual stops" to control the payout of the machines. Randomness was assured by the introduction of what became known as the Random Number Generator, or RNG. (More on this in Part Five.) These programs allowed the machines to accumulate enough play to make money for the casinos, while at the same time allowing for huge jackpots. Quickly, the public caught on and the slot era began.

No longer were players of slot machines looked down upon as silly people who needed to be kept amused while the real gamblers played the real games. With lightning speed, the slot machine took over the casino floor. While in years past, you would be hard-pressed to find a casino with more than one hundred slot machines, now you will be hard-pressed to find a casino with *fewer* than one thousand slot machines. Most of today's casinos have upwards of two thousand slot machines, with many casinos over three thousand, and some with even more than four thousand. Nationwide, about 80 percent of all casino revenue comes from slot machines. Little wonder that the slot player is now the most valued casino customer. Slot players are looked upon as a source of ready and steady income. This means, of course, that the slot players are looked upon as the perennial losers.

This does not have to be so. Slot players do not have to lose. There is information available which allows even the slot player an edge. Much has been written about casinos and casino gambling, and much has also been written about slot machines. Most of these writings conclude that slots cannot be beaten because they are games with a negative expectation. (More on this later.) But that's not quite so, for two reasons. One: Even a game with a negative expectation has to pay off sometime. If it did not, no one would ever play it; therefore, the casinos would never make *any* money, and therefore, the casinos would never have such a game. The trick is, consequently, to *find the machines which will pay the most, most often, and to play them under the most likely conditions of obtaining a winning sequence.* Two: By using slot clubs, choosing machines wisely, and employing several playing techniques, the slot player can gain an actual and real edge over the casino. Even more of an edge, in fact, on many occasions, than the best of the professional blackjack players. This will become more apparent as you read on.

Being a slot player no longer means being a loser. Slots can make you rich. Many of the giant progressives have made more than two hundred people multimillionaires. Many thousands of other slot players have had smaller but life-altering wins. And what of the tens of thousands, and even millions, of slot players who have won jackpots of $100, $500, $1,000, $5,000, and $10,000? There are hundreds of such winners in a single casino every day of the week. Sometimes every hour.

How do you get *your* share? Well, that's what this book is all about.

Preface

This book is part of a series called *Powerful Profits*. There are many very good reasons why this series of books is called just that. For two decades, I have worked in casinos, played in casinos, been a consultant to casinos and slot machine manufacturers, and spoken with tens of thousands of slot players and hundreds of casino executives and executives from the companies that manufacture the slot machines you play. I have been "inside" every slot machine on the casino floor. I have seen them in pieces, I have seen their motherboards and computer chips, I have seen the test data, called Par Sheets, I have been involved in the development, creation, manufacture, marketing, promotion, and actual use of the slot machine. From all this I have learned two important lessons:

1. If you don't know anything about slot machines, and still play them, you *will* lose.
2. If you learn the "what, why, where, when, and how" of slot machines, you *can* win.

So this book is really about these two revelations. There are many "secrets" about slot machines. The apparent simplicity of the device itself is highly misleading. Yes, the principle is easy to understand: Put a coin in, or multiple coins, pull the handle or push the buttons, the reels spin, come to a stop, and if you line up the winning combination, you win. If you do not, you lose. Simple, right? Well, not quite.

Modern slot machines are of many kinds and of varied evolutionary heritage. Machines manufactured by different companies may look the same or very similar, but that's merely an illusion. Many such machines are substantially different from others of their kind. Even machines made by the same manufacturer are not necessarily all the same, even though they may look identical. What separates these machines from each other is not so much the way they *look* in their outside cabinetry, but how they work on the *inside*. That's the first "secret" about slot machines.

Most people don't know that slot machines are entirely computer-controlled. All *modern* slot machines are computers, even if the machine may have reels and look like a mechanical slot machine. Even if the machine *feels* as if it has mechanical reels, it does *not*. It is still a computer, which runs on superfast microprocessors. To provide you with a comparison, think of the most expensive PC you can buy, with the fastest processor and the best and newest software. That will give you the best idea of what a slot machine really is. And that's the second "secret" about slot machines.

Okay, so now you know that slot machines are all computers, and that they aren't the same even if they look identical or similar. How do they work? Look inside your own computer, if you have one. If you don't have a computer, go to a computer store and ask them to show you a motherboard and a processor. You will see a lot of little silver dots and strings of metal all over the board. The processor looks like a spider with spokes, and it fits on a specific part of the motherboard. Plus, of course, there are a lot of cables and other stuff around, but that's not necessary for this example. That's the real slot machine. Just that. What you see there, the motherboard and the processor chip, is all the hardware that is required to have the basis for a slot machine. This is the computer *hardware*, as opposed to *software*.

Software is the programs that are generated to actually run the computer and make the game. These run on the operating system, which is made possible by the hardware on this motherboard and this processor chip. If you happen to be familiar with computers, then forgive me for this simplistic approach, but I want to make sure that everyone reading this can get an understanding of the basics of the hardware and software profiles of a slot machine. So now we have the hardware, the operating system, and the game software. These are the three essential components that make up a slot machine. So far, all of this is merely a display on a computer monitor, and it looks nothing like the slot machine you will find in the casino. That part of the manufacturing process involves the hardware cabinetry. This is where the steel, chrome, buttons, coin chutes, coin hoppers, bill acceptors, and Plexiglas "boxes" are added to the computer hardware, and the whole thing is made to look like the slot machine you will see in the casino. This then completes the machine, as we are accustomed to seeing it.

The final component is the game chip itself. This software program holds the actual game. This chip interacts with the other software and hardware components of the slot machine in order to render the accurate game which has been approved by the Gaming Regulatory Agency, or Regulatory Board, or whatever the government regulatory body may be in the state or country where the manufacturer seeks to have that game licensed for in-casino use. The game chip interacts with the graphics program, which renders the pictures you see on the reels (for video slots), or triggers the corresponding stops showing the pictures of the symbols on the machine's mechanical-looking reels. On these "reel" slots, the graphics program may not be necessary, because the physical reels themselves may still use the old-fashioned plastic strip with the winning combinations, and "ghosts," affixed to it, or printed on it.

Then there is something called the Random Number Generator, or RNG for short. This assures randomness in the generation of the binary numeric sequences that determine the final outcome of the spin, or event. Finally, an array of other components count the coins in, jackpots paid, coins out, number of spins, theoretical "hold," actual "hold," and a lot of information which is all but useless to the players but very important to the casino, and to the regulatory agencies which from time to time inspect the performance information of the machine and compare it to the approved statistical norms. So this is the third "secret" about slot machines.

How do they pay off? How do they make money for the casino? How do we know which ones are the better payers, and which ones are the "takers"? How do we find the good machines and stay away from the bad ones? Where in the casino should we play? Where do the casinos put their good machines, and where do they put the bad ones? How can we tell the difference between the different kinds of machines, if they look the same? Which manufacturer has the better games, and why? Which slot machine manufacturer should we look for as a brand name, knowing that they produce mostly good games that are fun to play and actually pay well? How should we play the machines to our best advantage? What strategy, if any, can we use to get the most value from our slot machine dollars? What about the bill acceptors? The slot clubs? What about comps? What about malfunctions? What about—well, I think we have asked enough questions.

These are the other "secrets" of the slot machines and how to play them to your benefit—and *that's why* this book. The game may seem simple. The questions may seem many.

The answers are all here. Some answers are simple, and some are not. But one thing is absolutely certain—if you don't know what is in this book, you can't make powerful profits from slot machines. You can be lucky, but luck is fleeting. To be a regular winner, to be able to go to a machine and know—really, actually *know*—that you have the best there is, and know how to play it to its fullest profit potential, and then know how to maximize your profits, and then know how to do this regularly and frequently, well, for that you can't rely just on luck alone. You need *knowledge*.

That's also *why this book*. So, without further delay, let us play and learn, so that we can learn to play for profit.

Introduction

The world of the casino is changing daily. This is especially true for the slot machines. Each day, new machines are introduced. Even as I write this, the newest crop of machines are being manufactured. Many of these will not be on the casino floor until 2004, or even later. The process involved in the manufacture of a slot machine is complex and lengthy. It is no longer as simple as making a box with three reels, each with ten stops on it, as it was when Charles Fey invented the Liberty Bell slot machine in 1895 and for some sixty years thereafter. Today's computer technology has fueled a boom in slot machine manufacture. As computers get faster, and as the capacity of the processors and memory chips gets bigger, more and more options are available for the software designer and the hardware engineer. There are now also numerous manufacturers, each competing for available casino floor space with their particular machine, brand, and game.

The process involved in getting a slot machine to your favorite casino begins with the concept for the game itself. More and more often, especially lately, these ideas for slot machines are what are commonly called "market identification" games. These are usually themed games based on something that is already popular or easily understood by the general public. For example, the *Wheel of Fortune*® game was ideally suited to a slot machine because of the success of the television show. The theme of the TV show was used in the manufacture of this machine, which is called a "hybrid" and is actually based on another slot machine called *Wheel of Gold*®.

Other games similar to these processes are also widely available. Among them are *I Dream of Jeannie*™, again based on a popular TV show, *The Munsters*™, likewise a TV show, *The Addams Family*™, based on popular cartoon characters, and numerous other new games, many of which I describe in Part Two. Some of these slot machines are already on the casino floor.

Once the idea is conceived, and the relevant rights obtained, the computer programmers and designers get together to actually work out how the game will play. Most of the time such new games are based on what is traditionally called the "existing game platform." What this means is that if the manufacturer already has a series of slot machines, some features of those machines can be used for the new game. Rather than having to design the entire program from scratch, the game is based on the existing play platform. Often merely the symbols on the existing game are changed; otherwise the game is identical to the one for which this original program was designed. This is how we get a series of games which have different themes and different symbols, but which have largely the same payoff programs and pay schedules. It's an inexpensive way to introduce what can be seen as a "new" game, although in reality the "new" part applies only to the theme and the graphics, while the actual program, or "meat," of the game is already on the approved platform. This also helps streamline the regulatory approval process.

However, not all new games are of this kind. Often the manufacturer actually has to start from the beginning, which involves the programming of millions of bits of information into the software programs to constitute an entire game program. This takes time, often many years. Then the cabinet has to be designed, the actual framework which holds the game. Meantime, the computer program and the chips are sent to a test facility. This facility "plays" the game by means of computer simulations for millions and millions of spins. This produces the statistics for how the game plays, and the true odds of the occurrences of each of the possible winning and non-winning combinations. This is then taken to the programmers, and the series of various "house withholding" percentage options are programmed (see Part Five for more details). More tests follow, resulting in a huge column of mathematical data, called a Par Sheet, which tells the entire story of the slot machine game. That information is then submitted to the regulatory agency or agencies which oversee the gaming regulations in each state or country where the manufacturer seeks licensing for this game, or for themselves as a licensed slot machine manufacturer. Upon initial approval, which normally happens after the board reviews the Par Sheets and compares that information with their own internally generated review, the game is sent for what is called a "field trial." This means that several of these machines will be installed in various casinos, so that real people can play them under real conditions. That's the final test, and the deciding test. If the people like the game, they will play it. If they don't, they won't. If the game "underperforms," meaning it doesn't match up to the expected player acceptance, the game usually dies right then and there, and the manufacturer goes back to the drawing board to come up with another game. If the game is accepted, but holds too much, or too little, for the casino, then alterations are made to the program to bring the game more in line with the theoretical expectations for the actual, and virtual, hold and payout percentages which are desired.

Finally, if all goes well, if the game is liked by the players, the regulatory agencies approve everything, and the casino take is good enough, then the manufacturer releases the game for general sales. Now it is up to the marketing and PR departments to sell this game not only to the public, so that they will play it, but primarily to the casinos so that they will place it on the casino floor and add it to what is called the casino's "slot mix." Each casino has the discretion to ask for a specific hold percentage. That's why even the same games can play differently, and pay vastly differently, from casino to casino (and sometimes, even in the same casino), because they don't all have to have the same payout and hold percentages.

Now the game is in many casinos, and people are playing it. How long it lasts depends on how long the people want to play it. And that is the final success story in the process of getting the slot machine to your favorite casino. The people who play them have the final say on whether the machine will be only a temporary success or become a permanent fixture among the standard slot mix of most casinos.

For these reasons and many other, listed in this book, it is important that slot players begin to grasp the various details of what slot machines are, how they are made, and how and why they are in the casino. Therefore, I begin this book with a short chapter titled "What Is a Slot Machine?" Even though we have already mentioned some of the details of what a modern slot machine is actually like, this short chapter will provide the most basic background and understanding of a game which looks simple but in reality is very complex.

Without this information, the rest of the details I wish to share with you—the "secrets," the answers to the most popular questions, and the more detailed descriptions of many of the most popular slot machines—may not make sense to you. That is why I have included it, even though I am aware that many of you will already know what a slot machine is. Or perhaps you only think you know. It could just be that your eyes and minds will become a little more open and a little more clear, even if some of the information in this first chapter may seem familiar. I invite you to discover this with me, from the very start. We can learn together, and have a lot of fun finding out.

Part One

HOW TO BECOME
A SMART SLOT PLAYER

What Is a Slot Machine?

The traditional slot machine is a mechanical, electro-mechanical, or computerized gambling device employing three, four, five, or more circular reels of varying dimensions. Each of these reels has several symbols either painted on, attached to it, or as video display symbols in video-based slots. These symbols can be anything at all, although the most common designs are cherries, bars, and—the jackpot symbol—the number 7. Whatever the symbol on the machine, it makes absolutely no difference to how the machine will play, or what and how much it will pay out. All these details are determined by the computer program carried by a tiny chip inside the machine's electronic brain. You could put pictures of your kids, rocks, spaghetti, cheese, or anything there, and if they lined up on the payline, you'd win the jackpot.

You begin play by inserting a specified number of coins or gaming tokens into a coin receptacle slot on the front of the machine, or by inserting currency into currency acceptors mounted on the machine, and then pulling the handle affixed to the right side of the machine or pressing the play button, either of which sets the reels spinning. The reels come to a stop in left-to-right order on the display screen (the window).

The object is to line up matching symbols (matching winning combinations) on the payline, usually a center stripe painted across the viewing screen on the traditional reel slots, or the virtual paylines on the video slots, usually shown in various bright colors. These can be viewed when pressing the button marked "paylines." The schedule of winning combinations is normally displayed on the front or just above the machine, or on the machine's video menu, accessible by touching the icon marked "pays," indicating the hierarchy of winning combinations and the amounts that each one pays whenever it appears on the active payline. Instead of a handle, most slot machines now employ a button marked "spin" which you press to start the reels turning. Like the handle, pressing it will spin the reels after the coin or coins are inserted.

Most modern slot machines also have a button marked "credit." Instead of paying off winners in coins, the machine will automatically credit any winnings to a credit meter. The credited winnings appear numerically on the machine's credit meter display, and, as an option, the player then has a choice of playing these credits or cashing them out. To play the credits, the player can press a button marked "play one credit," and for each time this button is pressed the machine will deduct one credit from the credit meter and register one corresponding coin as "coin in." The player may press this "play one credit" button up to the machine's maximum-coin limit. If, for instance, the machine you are playing takes three coins as maximum, you can press this "play one coin" button three times. These coins are then deducted from the player's credit meter and credited to the player's next pull. When this is done, the machine will usually say "coin accepted" on the display, or, in some cases, the paylines on the machine's display will light up. The effect is the same as if you had put three coins in the slot instead of using the credits you had accumulated.

Most of the modern machines also have another button called "play maximum coins," sometimes also identified as "play three coins" if that machine's maximum is three coins, or "play five coins" if that machine's maximum is five, and so on. By pressing this button, the player will automatically play the maximum coins which that machine takes. Newer video slots also have an icon marked "re-bet." If you touch this icon, the machine will automatically bet the same amount as was previously bet on the preceding spin, and play the next game. The player may cash out credits by pressing a button marked "collect." By pressing this button, or touching the appropriately identified video icon, the machine will pay out in coins, or gaming tokens, all the credits indicated on the credit meter. These coins then drop to the collection tray mounted at the bottom of the machine, or the machine will print out a collection ticket which can then be cashed at the change booth or casino cashier.

There are many different kinds of slot machines available in any casino. Don't get distracted by the apparent differences in symbols, styles, lights, or pictures. Practically all slots will play the same way, although their payoffs and frequency of payoffs will vary considerably from machine to machine, and from casino to casino. The symbols on these slots can be anything imaginable, although the number 7 is most often the primary symbol indicating top jackpots, with a combination of cherries and bars. These are the most common forms of graphic displays on slot machine reels, although many newer machines have such a wide variety of symbols that to list them here would be all but impossible, and certainly impractical. What is important to remember in all this is that the symbols themselves are quite incidental and mean very little—what *does* matter is what those symbols do, what they pay, and under which winning combinations. This you can find out by reading the payoff chart, usually mounted on or above the slot machine itself or on a separate video screen on the video slots, which you can access by touching the icon marked "pays." Modern slot machines, the ones found in virtually all major casinos today, are smooth, well-made, and brightly painted, with lots of lights and with catchy names like *Red, White & Blue*™, *Totem Pole*™, *Wild Cherries*™, and so on. Some are merely computer displays on a video screen, such as the slot machines found in multi-game machines, all of which are generally known as "video slots." The payoffs on any slot machine, whether a reel spinner or a video slot, are shown by the hierarchical scale clearly charted on the machine's pay-chart display.

Slots are the simplest game to play, although some of the more ambitious slots can look a trifle complicated. Don't get overwhelmed by the graphics, displays, or apparent complexity of a modern slot machine. No matter how complicated it looks, it works the same as every other slot machine. Line up the paying combinations on the win-line, and you win. Otherwise you lose. Some machines have more than one payline, and on these you can line up more than one pay at the same time. On some such machines, these pays add up; on others, only the highest payoff wins. Modern slot machines work on a computer program: random selection of winning combinations, based around a program command which determines the overall payout and take of such a machine over time. Winning percentages and odds are created by the manufacturer as part of the software program of the slot machine and are determined after millions of computer-simulated "spins." As with video poker, a modern slot machine will pay off the top jackpot after a certain number of spins and coins in. The number and frequency of such wins are determined by the payout percentage built into the program of that particular machine. Unlike video poker, however, the player has no choice in the matter and cannot affect the winning combinations. Slot machines are, therefore, a passive game, and not an interactive game. Although quite rare, there are some "second chance" reel slots, but these are not truly interactive in the same sense as video poker, and they are now mostly relegated to slot machine museums. On many video slots, the paylines which are active for that particular play will light up in various colors, and although you will not see them during the game, any winning paylines will show up and indicate the winning combinations on that win-line. You can tell which lines you have played by looking to the left, right, top, or bottom— depending on the available number of paylines—where you will usually see colored numbers from one to as many as the machine allows for maximum-coin play. For example, if your video slot machine has nine paylines, and you play them all, the numbers 1 through 9 will light up in various colors, thus indicating which paylines are now activated. And so on, for as many paylines as are possible on the machine which you happen to be playing.

Many people think that machines with certain symbols will pay better, and casino owners capitalize on this by offering theme machines. It's a popular concept. Some of these theme machines are the very popular *Red, White & Blue*™ 7s machines. These feature American patriotism. Others feature football, basketball, baseball, the jungle, fruits, animals, jokers, cards, and so on. This provides for a variety of looks, lots of bright lights, and lots of player excitement, but each is exactly the same as any other, with the *specific exception of their inherent program*. The point I'm making is this: Don't play a machine just because you like the symbols painted on the reels. Just because the *Red, White & Blue*™ machines, made by IGT, happen to be among the most "liberal," doesn't mean that you should select only machines with "patriotic" themes. You may wind up playing a machine which is *not* the IGT *Red, White & Blue*™, but only looks like it, and this could be a different experience for you. Understanding the importance of the symbols on the machine should *not* mean that you will seek out certain *themes*. Rather, it *should* mean that you will seek out *certain symbol combinations*, based on what you *know* are the *better-paying* combinations. Also, seeking out well-paying machines should mean that you look for the right brand, like the IGT games, because then you will *know* you have the right machine, the one for which you were looking, like the real *Red, White & Blue*™ game. All of this is important in your machine and game selection, as you will shortly discover.

Introduction to Reel Slots

The vast majority of all the reel slot machines found in any modern casino will be either 2-coin or 3-coin machines. This simply means that to win the top jackpot you must play the maximum coins, and the maximum number of coins these machines will accept on any one pull is either 2 coins or 3 coins per pull. You can easily tell which of these machines you are about to play by looking at the payoff win display on the screen mounted over the machine, or displayed on the machine's belly glass. Two coin machines will have the payoffs divided into two sections, the one on the left showing how much any winning combination of symbols will pay for a one coin play, and the one on the right showing what these same winning combinations will pay if 2 coins are played per pull.

You should always play the maximum coins. Here's why. In the case of a 2-coin machine, the winning combinations will often pay more for a 2-coin play than for a 1-coin play. This is particularly true for the top jackpot. On such a machine the second coin play may pay double what a 1-coin play would pay on the same winning non-jackpot combinations, but for the top jackpot, or maybe even the top two or three jackpots, the second-coin play will pay considerably more. For example, if the top jackpot payoff on a 2-coin-maximum machine is three 7s, paying, say, $1,200, the same three-7s combination will pay only $400 if you hit it with only 1-coin-in as your bet. This discrepancy in payoff amounts is an incentive for you to play the maximum coins, but it also offers an advantage to you. You will win considerably more money if you hit the required winning combination with maximum coins played.

These are a version of what are called the "buy-a-pay" machines, as opposed to simple "doublers." Buy-a-pay machines pay extra for maximum coin wagers. In effect, you are "buying the pay" for that extra payoff for the top jackpot, or the top two or three jackpot pays. The other kinds of machines are called doublers because they pay more for the extra coins wagered, but only double the pay for each extra coin bet. Among reel slots, most of the 3-coin machines are of that kind. These 3-coin machines work on the same principle. They may be exactly the same as their 2-coin counterparts, but their payoff schedules are divided into three sections on the payoff display. The first row indicates payoffs for winning combinations hit with 1 coin in, the second with 2 coins in, and the third with the maximum 3 coins in. As with the 2-coin-maximum machines, the 3-coin maximum-machine will show much higher payoffs for the top jackpots with the 3-coin maximum played on any one pull—*but* these 3-coin machines may also show what *look like* bigger payoffs for even the smaller pays. Be warned! Three-coin machines do not pay more for the smaller pays for the 3 coins because they are set to pay more. They pay more for these smaller pays because you have to *bet* more.

Unless the machine is a progressive, stay away from 3-coin slots. They will eat you up, even if it looks as though you are getting paid quite a lot. You will have a much better chance of walking away with some money if you play the 2-coin-maximum machines. By not spending that extra coin on a 3-coin machine, you will have more money to play with, which equals more pulls on that slot, which equals more chances to get the jackpot.

PLAY FOR THE PAY

Whatever slot machine you play, whether 2-coin, 3-coin, 4-coin, 5-coin, or whatever, *always play the maximum coins*. If you don't, you're shooting yourself in the foot. You will never make any significant money even if you win. By not playing maximum coins you take away from yourself the ability to cash in on the top-paying jackpot. It doesn't matter how many smaller pays you get. Even if you get them constantly you will almost never equal the amount that one pull can get you when you hit the top jackpot with maximum coins played. Always remember that many machines will pay the jackpot, or even a series of smaller pays, *only if you bet the maximum coins*.

Some slot machines show three lines in the pay window, but only the center line is marked as a "payline," usually by a stripe across the outside of the window. This means that to win anything, you must line up any winning combination on that center payline, and on that line only. There are also many machines that show three paylines: top, center, and bottom of the window. This means that any winning combination lined up correctly on any of the three paylines means you have a winner. The advantage of three-payline machines is that you get more smaller pays, sometimes even double and triple pays if winning combinations appear on two, or all three, paylines together. And on some machines you can get five or eight paylines or even more—*but* you have to bet more to activate them, so be very careful! Always check the payoff display first. The disadvantages in multi-payline machines are that the smaller payoffs are usually very small, much smaller than on one-payline machines, and also that the top jackpot is usually paid only if you line up the proper winning symbols in the correct sequence on the bottom, or third, payline. Or the fifth payline in case of the five-line machines, or the eighth payline in case of the eight-line machines, and so on—basically, *if you don't play all the paylines you cannot win the jackpot*!

Multi-payline machines may offer a graduated jackpot schedule, paying the smaller top jackpot for winning combinations lined up on the center line, more if they are lined up on the top, or second, payline, and the top award if they appear on the third, bottom, payline—or whatever that final payline may be. (In order not to further encumber this chapter, I will simply omit using the three-payline example for the *standard reel slots*, but you should note that the principles described for them are the same for all multi-payline machines, whatever number of paylines they may have. However, I should point out that although I tend to recommend against reel slots with three or more paylines, the situation is *exactly the opposite* on multi-payline video slots, where the advantage to the player lies directly in playing *all* the available paylines, regardless of the maximum-coin-bet requirements. More on this later.)

THE BEST REEL SLOTS

So which are the best reel slots? Probably the best reel slot machines to play are the double-up machines. An increasing variety of such machines employ "double-up" symbols. Typically these are circular symbols with the word "double" on them. Others can have a picture of a diamond with the word "double," as is the case with machines called *Dou-*

ble Diamonds™. Whatever the symbol is, if it says "double," this is the kind of machine to which I am referring.

The principle of this "double" symbol is very simple: Whenever it appears on the payline in combination with any other symbols which normally would have made a winning combination, the payoff amount is doubled. In most instances these "double" symbols also substitute for any other symbol. This means, for example, that if your machine is set to pay, say, 80 coins for three twin-bars, if you get two twin-bars along with a "double" symbol on the payline, you will be paid 160 coins instead of the regular 80 coins. As a further bonus, if you get two of the double symbols appearing on the payline with only one twin-bar, the winning combination is quadrupled. In my example, you will be paid 320 coins, instead of the regular 80 coins. You must be careful to see which machine you are playing. Not all machines will double and quadruple all pays, and not all machines will have a "double" symbol which also substitutes for any of the other symbols on the machine's reels. Some machines will have only two "double" symbols, one on each of the first two reels, while other machines will have three of these "double" symbols, one or more on each of the three reels. Also, some machines will have more than one "double" symbol on the first reel, but only one on the other one, or other two. However, most machines employing these "double" symbols will have one on each reel. On such machines the top jackpot is usually paid when you line up all three "double" symbols on the payline. In this case the top jackpot is paid as indicated on the payoff display and is not doubled or quadrupled further. But all other pays usually are.

When choosing one of these machines, it is important not to confuse them with "joker" machines, or "wild," or any other symbols noted on the machine's payoff display as being "wild." Symbols identified as being "wild" merely substitute for any other paying symbol, but do not always double the payoff. Similarly, on some machines that employ the "double" symbols, these "double" symbols may not substitute for other paying symbols. The best machine for you to play is one that has all the "double" symbols, where these symbols also substitute for any other symbol, and has a 2-coin maximum and a single payline. Machines that have only two of these "double" symbols, one on the first reel and one on the second reel, usually pay the top jackpot by combining both the double symbols in conjunction with a 7 on the third reel. These machines are just as good to play as those employing the three "double" symbols, providing it is a 2-coin maximum single-payline machine where these "double" symbols also substitute for other symbols.

Of all the various slot machines offered in casinos today, these kinds of machines will provide you with the most play, the best pays, and the best odds of hitting a top jackpot. The double-up symbols also offer bigger "small" jackpots when these smaller jackpots are hit in combination with one or two of the double-up symbols. Not so long ago there weren't many of these machines available at casinos, and you almost never would find them together in a single carousel. This has changed dramatically in recent times. Now there is a whole crop of slot machines which employ the "double" symbols, in various configurations.

MUlTI-PAY MACHINES

Also recently, there has been a new crop of machines called "triple" pay machines—mostly *"Triple Diamonds"*™, but what the symbols are doesn't matter—if it says "triple" on it, that's this kind of machine. These machines pay triple the winning combination if it is lined up with a single "triple" symbol as part of the winning combination, with such winning combinations paying nine times the regular payoff when two of the "triple" symbols appear on the payline with any other paying symbol. These machines play on exactly the same principle as their double-up counterpart, and are *highly recommended* as the best overall investment for your slot machine gaming dollars.

Among the newest slots are an ever-increasing variety of multi-pay machines. These are the natural evolution from the first-generation double and triple machines. On many of these machines, you will find pay symbols which will pay five times the payoff when one of these symbols is correctly lined up on the winning payline in combination with the correct symbols which would normally have constituted a pay. On these "five-times" machines, if you line up two of the "five-pay" symbols on the correct payline and with another symbol which is a paying symbol, this combination is then paid at twenty-five times the regular stated payoff for that combination without the two "five" symbols. On these machines the multi-pay symbols usually do not substitute for the other paying symbols, and therefore will pay only when correctly lined up with other combinations of symbols which would have been a standard non-bonus pay (see the payoff schedule on the machine to determine what these paying combinations are). However, the *advantage* is that if you do hit a pay, it is usually a very large one. And even the smallest-paying combination becomes significant when multiplied five times, and certainly so when multiplied twenty-five times. These events are "virtual jackpots"— meaning that although they are not identified as a "jackpot" on the payoff display, they nevertheless count as a jackpot because of the size of the win, when the win is so achieved with the use of these "extra pay" symbols.

You should be aware that, since these are, in effect, jackpots, they will not occur nearly as frequently as pays on, say, the double machine, or even the triple machines. These "hidden jackpots," as I call them, are factored in the program to which such machines play, and although they look inviting as a series of bonus-type pays when you look at the payoff display screen on the machine, they are not frequent enough to qualify for standard payoffs. It is for these reasons that you must consider these payoffs as "secondary" or even "tertiary" jackpots, and consequently not look to them to provide you with continuous "fuel" for your play—as is mostly the case with the double machines. On the double and triple machines, for example, you get paid even for the hit of a single bonus symbol, since they mostly also substitute for all other symbols. In these instances you get paid for having achieved the minimal pay (cherries usually), plus the bonus pay for having done so with the use of these bonus symbols. This accounts for significantly more hits and more pays, which directly translates into longevity of play and lower required playing budget.

There are some multi-pay machines, particularly many of the video slots, where the multi-pay bonus symbols actually substitute for the majority of other pay symbols. If you can locate one of these machines, they are also among the best slot machines to play, primarily because the playing principles and required budget are similar to those for the double or triple machines. There are also other kinds of multi-pay machines that have bonus symbols which do not substitute for other symbols, but do double (or otherwise multiply) the pay. These machines have another "bonus" symbol which does substitute for all other symbols, but does not double (or otherwise multiply) the pay. These are the "multi-pay-multi-bonus" machines, and the use of this secondary "substitute" symbol becomes significant, because you can now achieve more frequent pays, including more frequent multi-bonus pays, than on machines which do not have either the "substitute" option for the "multi-pay" symbol or the secondary "substitute" symbol. These machines then also become a viable candidate for your gaming investment, but you should be aware that these "second-ary substitute" symbols do not always double the pay, nor act as the primary multi-pay symbol; they merely substitute for all other symbols, as a "wild" symbol would. In fact, most such uses of the secondary substitute symbol are called "wild," and although I have previously advised against playing machines with only "wild" symbols, in this case—and this case only—the use of these "wild" symbols is beneficial, because you can achieve many more paying combinations than without them, and do so more frequently in combination with the multi-pay bonus symbols.

In the final analysis, the advantage to you as the slot player is in the longevity of your play versus the expendi-ture required, which equals the opportunity to hit a signifi-cant pay.

This simple formula works well on these multi-pay ma-chines, as it does on the double and triple machines when you are calculating your potential profit relative to size of bankroll and expected play frequency. In fact, this simple formula is worth noting for any slot play, and in fact for any gambling activity, whether on slots, tables, or any other casino game.

I would also like to point out that among the newest reel slots there are machines called *10 Times Pay*™, and even *12 Times Pay*™, and other such machines which have bonus symbols which multiply the pay, called "multipliers." All of these kinds of machines are the evolutionary products based on the oldest "double-up" machines I already men-tioned. As with the *Five Times Pay* ™ machines, these ma-chines also offer these virtual jackpots, but they are just as difficult to hit as the five-times machine. The infrequent oc-currence of hits with one or more of these multiplier sym-bols present in a winning event is the greatest detractor from playing them. However, *the converse is also correct*. When *getting* a hit with one or more of these multiplier symbols present, the award is *substantial*. So the balance is really there. As a player you must decide whether you wish to play a machine with more-frequent hits, smaller pays, and smaller jackpots, or take a shot at getting bigger pays with bigger payoffs but with less-frequent hits. The choice is yours.

I prefer my money to last longer, and I am quite satisfied with a win several times the amount of my bankroll or session investment. I tend to advise players to seek out machines with greater hit frequencies rather than taking the long shots on these many-times multiplier machines. But this doesn't mean that I am asking you to stay away from them. It simply means that I recommend that you budget your play. If you get lucky, so be it. If not, you still have the majority of your bankroll or session stake available and can go on playing on the more frequently hitting machines I described earlier.

CAROUSELS

Many slot machines of all kinds can also be found in what are called carousels. A carousel is an arrangement of several slot machines, either in a circle, an oblong, or some other combination which distinguishes these slot machines as a group. The machines can even be arranged in groups called "slot islands," although technically they can still be called carousels. Sometimes these carousel machines may be linked together for a progressive, and in this case the principle is the same as for any other kind of progressives. Most often, however, carousels are made up of several different kinds of machines simply grouped together.

Carousel machines are usually mixtures of the 2-coin and 3-coin single- and three-payline machines. The good machines I spoke of earlier are normally found somewhere in the middle of a group of other machines, or singularly

relegated to some obscure part of the casino. The philosophy behind this is also well thought out. Casinos know
which machines pay better than others (the "double-up"
machines particularly). So if they put one among a group of
machines that do not normally pay as well, people will be
attracted to that group of machines if they see one player
cleaning up on the good one. Other players will think the
rest of these machines also pay as well, and proceed to play
them. Similarly, by putting one of these good machines in
an area of the casino not normally frequented by players, the
casino will maximize profit per square foot of floor space, by
attracting players to that area of the casino floor when they
see a smart player winning on that good slot machine.
Lately, there has also been a trend among casinos to place
small slot islands of very loose slots in some highly visible
area, but away from the table games. These are usually islands of between four and six slot machines, which are set
as loose as the casino wants to make them. They are so
placed because they can be seen from many different areas
of the casino, as well as by passers-by. People who play
these machines tend to win more pays more often, and the
general joy which this elicits from these players, and often
also from passing people congratulating the lucky player,
have a direct and positive effect upon other people. These
other people may be motivated to try their own luck, and
may play machines elsewhere in the casino whose programs
may not be nearly as good as for those in the slot island.

Don't be afraid to walk around the casino and look for
the good slot machines. Give yourself a chance to win by
applying your new knowledge toward making more informed choices. A word of warning: Don't automatically expect that you will win, even on such machines. I call them
"good" machines because, relatively speaking and in comparison with most of the others, all play and payoff factors
being considered, they offer the player the best chance at

winning something, even if this is merely a series of smaller pays that keep you going. But it is still a chance. You are still gambling, and this means you can also lose. But your chances of *not* losing are better on these kinds of machines than on the others, and that is why I call them "good."

SLOT CYCLES

As I said before, modern slot machines are computerized and their payoffs are set by computer software programs. But slots still run in cycles, especially so since the winning selections are made at random by the slot machine's computer program. The machine's randomization program, usually referred to as the RNG (Random Number Generator), scans the possible winning combinations in microseconds. There are literally billions of possibilities. When you insert the first coin or play the first credit, the scan stops, and whatever combination was selected will be the one you'll get.

In the end, the slot machine will invariably average its take and payout per the program at which it is set. But all slots run hot and cold from time to time, and there are the inevitable short-term trends one way or the other. Even if you are playing one of the machines I call "good," you may hit the machine at a time when it takes. When this happens, the machine is in the off cycle. Other times you can play a bad machine, and it will shower you with coins. That one is in a pay cycle. This is a *very simple* way of describing it. The reality is mathematically complex, but it comes down to largely the same thing. Sometimes the machines will pay out far *more* than their mathematically preprogrammed percentage, and other times a lot *less*. So we call this the pay cycle, and the converse the take cycle. This may be colloquially convenient, but it's also quite accurate in the real world of in-casino slot play.

As you play slots, you will see what I mean by cycles. All of a sudden any given machine can start paying like it's raining money. And then, just as fast, it can stop. The trick is in recognizing when you are in a pay cycle and when you are not. Sounds easy, but it isn't. There is no way of telling how long a pay cycle will last, or how long a take cycle may last. If you play a specific slot machine for several hours, you will experience a few of these fluctuations, but when you hit an actual pay cycle, you'll never forget it. Suddenly it will appear that you can do no wrong. If you're lucky enough to hit one of these cycles, try to be smart enough to recognize it. Rake in the money, and keep a sharp eye for a downturn. A lot of machines will ease out of a pay cycle by teasing you with "almost there" pays, mostly by showing you an "almost" big jackpot. When this happens it's time to take your money and run. Chances are this machine will eat up all your winnings and then some. But if you have played a while and racked up quite a stack of coins, and the machine is still paying, keep playing it. But stop when you suddenly start to see the machine showing you these "almost" pays, especially when it starts showing you "almost" top jackpots. Take your money and try another machine. The machine which has started to show you the "almost" pays and "almost" jackpots will eventually hit the top jackpot (as all machines eventually do), but it is more likely to eat up the money it paid you before it does, and then it can eat up even more of your own money before the top jackpot happens. This is a sign of warning, because typically you will hit the top jackpots quite unexpectedly. Most of the time you will not hit the top jackpots when the machine is showing you "almost" jackpots, but when it is *not* showing any "almost" combinations for the top jackpot, but still manages to pay you smaller pays along the way. The old adage "You get it when you least expect it" applies here.

Machines appear to run in cycles. Sometimes the machine is hot, which means it pays out a lot and pays often. At other times, the machine is cold, which means it doesn't pay out much of anything at all. This seems to be a common perception among just about every slot player I know, myself included. I have also read this in many books on slots, and on casino games which include slot machines. If we were going to discuss table games, this would be called "trends." In blackjack, for example, we can easily use a method called the "tracking of the trends." Basically, this is kind of like keeping a sharp eye on what is happening with the decks, the game, or the shoe. Sometimes the cards are in our favor. Other times they favor the house. Still other times it is one for us and one for the house, almost even, with neither the players nor the house seeming to have any kind of trend in any direction.

With slot machines the trends appear far more pronounced. "Appear" is the key word here. We, as human beings, have a tendency to look for patterns in nature. That's one of the major reasons we like slots so much. The object of lining up a winning *pattern* is what makes us psychologically satisfied. However, there is no denying that in the real world, trends *do* occur. In fact, many strategies for casino games are based in the recognition of positive and negative trends. In slot machines, we call them cycles. Yet many people, even some gaming writers, deny that there is anything like cycles. This seems strange to me. I have no desire to dispute the mathematical basis for the randomness of slots, other than to point out that nothing made by man can be truly random. In fact, I have some questions about the often-quoted mythical RNG. (More on this later.) To my mind, slot cycles are as real as any trend in any gambling game and, indeed, any trend in nature. Sometimes we get more hurricanes and twisters than at other times. These are weather trends, sometimes called weather patterns. Of course, if you know your weather, and happen to be informed about global weather patterns and phenomena such as El Niño, for example, then these trends in weather will not be nearly as big a surprise to you as to others who may not have this information. This also applies to slot machines, and to gambling games in general. The more information you have, the more you are empowered to recognize patterns and trends. And this can lead you to better wagering decisions and more winners.

In slot machines, cycles can appear very pronounced at times, while at other times it is hard to tell if the machine has any cycle at all. Although mathematically and statistically, cycles are indefinable, and mostly the realm of the player's psychological perspective, there is nonetheless physical proof that machines, like cards or dice, run in groups of sequences. Although in the very long run these statistical anomalies will eventually even out, at least reasonably so, the truth is that in the short term the statistical probability of any slot machine running hot or cold is equally plausible. Trends or cycles contrary to the overall expected probability—or in the case of slot machines, contrary to the overall payback programming—do happen in all gambling games, and slot machines are no exception.

Much that is written in gambling literature has a lot to do with cautioning people against expecting the reality of the world to exactly mirror the theoretical percentages. Usually, this is done with examples such as this: If the machine's program indicates that it pays out 98 percent, this means that over the lifetime of that machine, its payout percentage will equal that 98 percent program, or at the very least be within statistically acceptable norms. This does *not* mean, dear slot player, that for every $100 you put into this machine you will always get back $98.

Without going further into these discussions, this example does make the point. Nothing in the real world exactly mirrors the statistical model. What actually happens is that

sometimes when you put your $100 into such a slot ma-
chine you will get paid back a lot *more* than your $100, and
this means that the machine is giving you back far more
than its programmed payback percentage. Conversely, at
other times the machine will pay you back at far *less* than
the programmed payback percentage. This simply means
that sometimes the machine will be hot and sometimes it
will be cold. In the end, both extremes will equate sufficiently so that the overall statistics for that machine's program are equal to, or reasonably equal to, the programmed
98 percent payback. Therefore, spotting trends in gambling,
and likewise cycles in slot machines, is one of the key skills
that will assist you in your playing success. If a slot machine
is paying you more than the money you put into it to start
your play, then this one is giving you back far more than its
program indicates. This one is in the hot cycle. When it
isn't, then it's in the cold cycle. These are just expressions
we use to help us understand these statistical anomalies in
the overall life of that machine's program.

How do you find out which machine is in which cycle?
Well, you have to test them with your play first. There are
several methods you can use. One of them is to start with a
set amount of money, say $100 for a $1 machine which takes
2 coins as maximum. This will give you fifty total pulls with
your original $100 investment. Run the money through the
machine, and then look at your credit meter and see what
you have left. Do not play your wins. Just add them up. If
your wins are at more than your starting amount, you may
indeed have a hot machine. Cash out, keep the profit, and
do it again. If you again have more than you started with,
then you have a hot one. Do it again. And again. Keep doing
it as long as you are ahead, or no more than $20 behind, at
any one session. Once you start to see the trend to the opposite, namely that you are starting to lose more than $20 per

session, and this happens twice, leave this machine. It's turning cold. Then go and do this again on some other machine. This way you will never actually lose your starting stake, will make lots of plays, and will give yourself the best chance at the highest jackpot.

DENOMINATIONS

Slot machines used to take pennies, nickels, and dimes. Now you will almost never find a penny machine or a dime machine, unless it is in a museum or a novelty attraction part of a casino promotion. (With the exception of some of the newest multi-denominational video slots, which can be played for as low as a penny per credit. However, some of these machines take as many as 250 credits per pull, so they aren't *really* the olden-style penny machines after all. The same applies to the "dime" machines, because these are just choices from the multi-denominational menu.) Most of the machines you find on the general casino floor use nickels, quarters, $1 tokens, and $5 tokens as denominations for play. You will also find some selections of half-dollar machines, but most half-dollar slots you find will be video poker machines, not reel slots. In reel slots, you will mostly find machines that take $1 tokens, $5 tokens, $10 tokens, $25 tokens, $100 tokens, and occasionally $500 tokens.

It used to be that quarter players comprised the majority, and dollar players were prized by the casinos as among their best customers. Like inflation, everything goes up, and so do player expectations. These days it is the $5, $10, and $25 slot player who is considered to be the best kind of slot player for the house. Consequently, an ever-increasing variety of $5 and higher-denomination slot machines are hitting the market, known as "high-end" slots, or "high-roller" slots.

HIGH-ROLLER SLOTS

These machines are mostly 2-coin, three-reel, single-payline regular slots, and even progressive slots, and many employ the "double" symbols we discussed earlier. These machines are by far the best machines around. Because of the simple numbers formula of the average relative loss expectation per player per pull, many casinos often order their loosest machines in these higher denominations. You can win a lot on them, but you can also spend a lot. If your bankroll isn't $2,000 or more, don't even think of sitting down at a $5 slot machine. Many $5 slot players I know will go through $3,000 to $5,000 per hour playing them, and that is not even counting the small pays they get and put back in. But you can be lucky. I saw a young man at Caesars Palace play just two $5 coins in a slot machine at Caesars High End VIP slot area and win $18,000! It can happen. But on the average, playing any slot machine can be a grind, and you must have time and money available to last out the cycle until you get something worthwhile. Regular $5 slot players know this and have enough money to keep playing until they get a decent win. Even a small pay on a $5 slot machine pays in the thousands.

Of course for the real high rollers, casinos like Bellagio, Caesars Palace, Bally's, Las Vegas Hilton, Luxor, MGM Grand, the Mirage, Golden Nugget, Paris, and Mandalay Bay, as well as many others in Las Vegas and elsewhere, offer the $25, $100, and $500 slots. Needless to say, if you plan on playing any of these machines, you'd better have plenty of handy cash, or a substantial credit line at the casino cage! It is hard to believe that anyone would actually play a $500 slot machine, but there are people who do. Two players at Caesars Palace are renowned for this kind of play. Caesars sends their corporate jet to get them, wherever they may be, when they wish to come there.

Many players like this frequent Las Vegas, and many more players frequently play the $25 and $100 machines. Even more surprising, is the fact that the casinos do not make most of their slot wins from these players. With the amounts of money these people gamble regularly you'd think the profit for the casino would come from them, but that is not the case.

HOW AND WHERE THE CASINO MAKES MONEY FROM SLOTS, AND WHY THIS IS IMPORTANT

Most of the casino's profits from slot play comes from the nickel and quarter players. Not even from the dollar slot player! The reasons for this are quite logical.

The VIP slot players, $1, $5, $25, $100, and $500 players, usually enjoy comps: freebies. To keep them coming back, the casinos offer these players free rooms, free food, free drinks, free shows, and even free airfare. And the machines these people play are almost entirely the best-paying machines available, the most liberal slots. The casinos' take on these slots is lower overall, and coupled with the comps handed out to these players, the casinos' profit margin per machine and per player is quite low.

They make up for this on the quarter and nickel players. Quarter and nickel players are mostly the casual crowd, who generally have no idea what kind of slots to play and how to play them, how to choose them, and all the other information I am sharing with you here. These nickel and quarter reel slot players may gamble $100 to $1,000 each per trip, as opposed to maybe millions of dollars for a $500 player, or several thousand dollars for the $1 and $5 players, but there are many more of them. Further, the regular reel nickel slot machines are the worst-paying machines under the sun, and the quarter slot machines are only marginally better. If you want to play nickels or quarters, play *video* slots, or the kinds of reel slots I recommend. (See Part Two.) These will offer you better odds, better pays, and typically longer playing time than other kinds of reel slots in the same denominations.

If you really want to play the *traditional style reel slots*, your best bet is to play $1 or $5 machines. If you have $100 to gamble with, you'll be better off playing video slots than quarter or nickel reel slots. If you have $1,000 to gamble with, you are far better off playing *dollar* reel slots than quarter reel slots. Dollar reel slots, $5 reel slots, and their higher-dollar versions are a better investment for your gaming dollar.

ADVERTISED PAYBACK

So what do "98 percent return," "Payback of 97.4 percent," "Most liberal slots in town," and all such other forms of advertising mean?

Generally speaking, playing a carousel of slot machines advertised as "98 percent return" is better than playing machines advertised as "94 percent return." One does not need to be a mathematician to see this. However, when applied to slot machines, this does not ordinarily mean that you will win more on the machines advertised as "98 percent return" than on those advertised as "94.7 percent return." Advertising can often be deceptive (sometimes unintentionally). There are two main factors to consider, as this applies to casino advertising for slot machine pays, regardless of whether this advertising is in newspapers, magazines, or displayed in the casino in neon lights:

One: If a casino advertises specific slot machines as "98 percent return," this will *never* mean that for each $100 you put into any one slot machine you will get back $98. A lot of first-time players make this mistake and it causes them anguish and confusion. What this *does* mean is that *over* *the life cycle of that particular slot machine*, it will *average* payoffs equivalent to 98 percent of all the money put through it, or as close to this percentage as is statistically possible.

All slot machines have counters inside them. These are tiny numerical displays hidden inside the machine, and they count each coin put in and each coin paid out. In addition, when the machine hits a jackpot which is paid by hand by the attendant, this person fills out a pay order. This pay order is like a paycheck, and is the document used by the attendant (usually the casino floorperson) as verification of the jackpot and authorization to go to the casino cashier and get the money to pay the winner. On this pay order are all sorts of interesting items that are completed for accounting information: the number of the slot machine, its code, the day and time the jackpot hit, number of coins played and how many coins played were registered so far on the "coins in" meter inside the machine, and so on. Some casinos now even use an automated computerized system that works on the same principle as the bar codes you see on your purchases at the supermarket. In these casinos the floorperson will take out a wand which emits a laser—like the automated supermarket checkouts—scans a predetermined series of bar codes, and identifies and records that particular machine and its payoff information. This information is, in the final tally, added to that machine's drop (coins in). When all is done and tallied at the end of the fiscal year, that machine's coins paid out will equal 98 percent of all the coins put in—including all the cash hand-paid jackpots throughout the year—*if that machine was set for the 98 percent payback*. Such payoff percentages are part of the computer program inside that machine which determines the final payoff average.

Many casinos now also use an even more recent system which is a direct computerized link to the cage, or change booth, through a master computer. When a jackpot hits, that information is either automatically sent to the main computer, which prints out the jackpot ticket, or the floorperson comes over to your machine, inserts a card into the slot club card reader, and presses a series of codes. This then sends the information to the main computer. This helps to speed up the process of paying winners, but it also helps the casino keep track of how that machine is performing. When it comes time to do the machine's accounting, upon review or general verification, this computerized data already displays that information. On virtually all of the video machines, this function is already part of the system. It simply reads and displays all of this information, and can be accessed by a coded key and by the proper menu commands from a selection accessible only to an authorized casino employee. All of this makes it easier to know what is happening with any machine on a daily and even hourly basis if the casino wishes to check the data. In some casinos, this data is downloaded either automatically by the machine directly to a central computer, or by casino employees with a portable computer which downloads the information, which is then transferred to the central computer for analysis. That's how casinos keep track of whether they are making or losing money on any machine.

Two: Even if a casino advertises "98 percent return" over a bank of several slot machines, or a carousel, this does not necessarily mean that *all* the machines in that carousel are set to pay off at those rates. To comply with advertising fair practice laws and gaming regulations, the casinos are only required to have one machine that is set to pay back 98 percent of the drop. The rest of the machines can be set at 94 percent, for example, or maybe even lower. A few years ago one casino advertised 101 percent payback on their machines, but they had only two of these in the whole casino.

Of course, it is in the interest of the casino to have players winning on such machines because it allows for player excitement, a lot of yelling, happy people, and good publicity. In defense of the casinos, I would vouch that almost all who advertise these "98 percent return" or "97.4 percent payback," and so on, actually do have all their machines in such carousels set to those advertised payoffs. The logic behind this is simple again. If people see other people winning, they will think this casino has good machines and go to play there as well. Even if all the machines in that casino paid at that 98 percent rate, the casino would still make the 2 percent end-of-the-year profit. With an average of over 1,000 slots per casino, even the 2 percent profit on slots still allows the casino to "win" around 80 percent, or more, of their overall profits from slot machines. But as a player, you are not interested in the long-term grind of small profits. You are interested in a good time and a fair shot at winning a jackpot.

You should also watch out for advertised slogans which say things like "up to XX percent payback." Whenever the words "up to" are part of that message, the casino may not have all their machines set at this rate; the payback is "up to" that percentage. What this really means is that most of the machines may be set at paybacks far lower than that advertised payoff, while only a few machines are set at that payoff, or higher. So if you play these machines and are lucky to catch the one which pays the advertised payoff, or better, then you have the best that casino offers. However, the fact will be that all of the other machines may not be set at that precise payoff percentage and may, in fact, be set substantially lower. Be very wary any time you see any display which says "up to" whatever percentage payback that shows.

Casinos make money in several ways:

• They offer machines with lower paybacks among the lower-denomination machines, such as nickels and quarters.

- They offer incentives to $1, $5, and higher-denomination players, because they know that these players will spend *more* per hour than the nickel and quarter players. Attracting these players will have the end result that the casino will make more money in the long run, even though it may be paying out a little more to some players in the short term.
- By carefully positioning slot machines in various areas of the casino, they will attract players either to underperforming areas or to more machines by having some set at very loose payoffs, such as the slot islands mentioned earlier.
- By advertising popular payoff percentages, but not necessarily having all the machines set at those rates, they will make more money from the players who weren't lucky enough to sit at the better-paying machines.
- Regardless of the payoff percentages advertised, and regardless of how loose the machines are, the final, undeniable fact remains that any game which is *set* to pay back *less* than 100 percent of the money invested in it *will always make money for the owner of that game.*

In the final analysis, that is how and why the casinos can, and do, offer all these wonderful varieties of slots— because they will always win on all of them in the long run.

Does that mean you should never play slots? Of course not! It simply means that you should know what you are getting and be prepared for it, and play accordingly. All slots have to pay something. If they didn't, nobody would play them and there would be no casinos as we know them. You *can* walk away with some extra money, by knowing how to play and how to choose the machines you will play. I have written this book, and the others in this series, to share the secrets, so that you know how to handle these games when you go to the casinos. Now you too will be able to "play the percentages."

PERCENTAGE PLAY

A percentage player is a smart slot player. If you keep your eyes open and your mind clear, your visit to the casino will be enjoyable and, very possibly, profitable. Many astute slot players will sit or stand near their favorite carousel and watch what's happening. After a while they find a machine that has had considerable play—but proportionally few pay-outs—and only then begin to play it. This is more discipline than superstition. Players who practice this tend to feel that the machine is "due" if it's been played a lot and hasn't paid a jackpot. Playing slots in the wee hours of the morning also seems better, around 1:00 A.M. to 7:00 A.M. Not only will you find a greater selection of machines, since most people do not stay up all night, but you are more likely to pick up machines that have had extensive play the evening before. Logically, the greater selection you have, the greater the possibility that you will find a machine that will pay off. Some players simply walk up and down rows of slot machines and put the maximum coins in all of them as they walk by. Often they catch one that pays a jackpot on that first pull! This is not necessarily the best way to play, particularly if you paid attention to what you have read thus far and now know how to select the better machines and play them to your optimum advantage. To summarize, I offer you the following guidelines, designed to help you in your slot play:

1. Select a casino offering 94 percent or better payback on its slot carousels.
2. Play only the $1 or the $5 (or higher-denomination) *reel* slots, and stay away from nickel and quarter *reel* slots altogether. (The reason I have italicized the word

"reel" is because I want to make certain you understand that this piece of advice applies *only* to the *standard reel* slot machines, and not to the newest multi-line video slots. On these newest video slots the playing principles are far different, and we will explore that a little farther on.)

3. Visit the casino and observe the slot play. If the machines are busy, and their current slot players are winning, it is a good bet that you too can find a machine there that will give you good play and possibly offer you a win, large or small.

4. Look for slot islands in highly visible areas. These tend to be the best-paying machines in the casino.

5. Don't try to "push your bet." If the machine pays off, manage your money. It is better to take a break with a little profit to play again than to lose it all and try to get it back by investing more money in that same machine. If your machine does hit the top jackpot, chances are it won't hit it again (or much of anything else for that matter) for quite some time. If this happens, take your money and move on.

IMPORTANT HINT

One crucial piece of information you should always remember for any slot machine, whether reel slot or video slot is this: Before you play, look at the payoff display screen on the machine and carefully read all the information there. This will tell you not only how the machine is set to play, but which combinations pay what and under which conditions. Look to see if the "extra bonus" pay symbols also substitute for all other symbols, or whether they do not. Also determine whether these "extra bonus" pay symbols are "wild" and whether they pay even if they appear "scattered"—meaning one off the payline, either above or below, or anywhere in the window (or the screen). The best combination machine to play is one where the "extra bonus" pay symbols not only substitute for all other symbols, but also pay the bonus in addition to being wild when they show up with other paying combinations, and also pay if they appear scattered, including pays when the scattered function combines with any other paying symbols on the primary win-line.

The combination of "extra bonus" + being "wild" + also substituting for all other symbols + paying the "bonus" in any winning combinations + also paying when "scattered" + also paying win-line "near miss" pays and paying them with the bonus is rare. The kind of machine you want to play is one where the *majority* of these features apply to that machine. This you can find out by paying close attention to the information on the machine's payoff display screen. This is usually written in small letters, but it is there. In this way, you will be able to select the best possible pay structure and therefore give yourself the most chances at a good win.

The Good, the Bad, and the Ugly

With apologies to Sergio Leone, the famed movie director who brought us those Clint Eastwood "spaghetti" westerns, this moniker certainly seems to apply to the vast variety of slot machines you will find in the casinos. Indeed there are some very good machines, some very bad ones, and certainly some which can only be described as downright ugly. Not necessarily because of the way they look, although some of these machines are made in cabinets which *are* ugly.

Most of the time when I refer to a "good" machine, I mean that this is one of the better games you will find. Sometimes I will actually identify a particular machine, as I did earlier when I mentioned the *Double Dollars*™ machines I liked so much several years ago. The general classification of "good" which I give to these machines means that they have at least the *majority* of my following "Top Ten" characteristics:

1. The game is simple to play and understand.
2. It offers a good variety of pays.

3. It pays frequently, and even the small pays amount to more than the base bet.

4. It has a graduated pay scale, with at least the top jackpot paying extra for maximum-coin play, and preferably the top two or three jackpots as well. This puts the majority of these machines in the "buy-a-pay" classification, but that's not necessarily bad.

5. It offers "multiplier" symbols which also substitute for all other symbols, or at least it has "wild" symbols along with the "multiplier" symbols. I prefer those which simply have the "multiplier" symbols which substitute for all others, but it's a toss-up. Some of the "wild + multiplier" machines can be very good payers. Others may not. I personally tend to prefer the "bonus + match + multiplier" machines, where those special symbols perform all these functions.

6. It has a generous bonus structure which actually hits often enough to be worthwhile.

7. It offers sizable pays and frequent hits on scattered pays. This is more important for video slots than the reel slots, but it does apply to a range of both kinds of machines.

8. It has a payback percentage program of at least 94 percent minimum. I actually prefer to search out the 98 percent machines among the reel slots. These can be easily found in most casinos. Among the video slots, and other games such as slot hybrids, the payback percentages are not that easy to determine, but it is possible to make some good choices. (More on this later.)

9. It has ticket printers rather than coin hoppers, or at least it offers both options depending on the amount of the payout. It is mounted in a cabinet with easy

buttons, and is not sitting too high so I don't have to reach up to play it.

10. Finally, it is any kind of machine that does *not* have fixed seating in front of it. I absolutely *hate* machines which have fixed seats in front of them, because they are usually so badly designed that you can't play the game comfortably. As a possible 10(a), I also hate machines with small coin trays, or hard-to-reach coin drop pits, which is a distinct problem particularly on the slant-top machines.

Well, there it is: Vic's Top-10 list (with apologies to David Letterman). It may not be nearly as funny as his, but it is appropriate for what we are discussing. I will now explain in more detail what I mean by each of the items in this list and exactly what I mean by a "good" slot machine.

THE GOOD
Easy to Play and Understand

For a machine to be classified as "good" in my list of preferences, the game should be easily understood, and the machine should be easy to play. Some of the newest reel slots contain such a variety of symbols and pays that often it isn't immediately apparent what pays what, under which circumstances, and for how much. This makes it harder to make a valuing decision when considering your gaming investment.

Some other reel machines are what is called a "hybrid," which means that they are connected to another feature which is triggered by a specified symbol or combination of symbols on the base game. On some of these games it is not immediately apparent which symbols do this, and what constitutes the primary and secondary jackpot on the base game, what is the best jackpot on the bonus game, and, if the machine is also a progressive, what wins the top progressive jackpot. Also, it is often not easy to determine whether any of these symbols substitute for the others, or are wild, or act as scatters. This can get very confusing. Yes, it is true that most of the popular slots aren't really hard to figure out, but there are enough of these confusing machines out there to warrant this segment.

Eventually you will be able to figure all this out, but usually you will have to start playing the machine first and find out as you play. This can cost you money. Even though most of this information is usually displayed on the machine (somewhere), often these explanations aren't clear enough or visible enough. You may think this is one kind of a machine, because it looks familiar, and you start playing it only to discover that this machine is different. This process of discovery has now cost you money, and it was not necessary. Those machines which I call "good" make it easy for you to find out. They have clear displays and show information you can find almost immediately, without having to look and investigate further. Some of the newest machines, and even some of the current and older ones, often pack so much information and so many game options into the machine that this information becomes harder to find. Also, many of the machines use large areas of their outward display for advertising and incentive purposes, leaving little room for game information.

This situation tends to get a lot worse on the video slots. These have such a huge variety of game, bonus, line, and play and pay options that it is just about impossible to find all this out without some intensive research and reading. Unfortunately, I can't write about every machine you may encounter, but the information I do present here should enable you to make better decisions, and make it possible for you to at least know where to look and what to look for. On the video slots, there are also "help" and "pay" screens, and these can be quite helpful to you in finding out how this machine plays and what it pays and how. This is very important information for you to know before you ever make an investment in the game. Unfortunately, this information can often be very confusing and not well-written. Among the machines I call "good" are those whose play features can be easily recognized and quickly identified and whose games, bonuses, and pay structures are likewise easily seen and understood.

Good Variety of Pays

This can be simple or complex, but if the pays are easily understood and their function can be clearly seen, it doesn't matter if there are only a few or many. Some of the reel slots fall into this category, because their pay structure is so simple. For example, the double-up machines may have cherries, a single bar, a double bar, a triple bar, and the "double" symbols multipliers. And that's it. Very simple, very clean. With a simple glance at the machine's payoff information, you know exactly what pays what, when, and how. There are a variety of these kinds of machines, be they doublers, triple-pays, five-time pays, ten-time pays, or more, or whatever. Other kinds of reel machines are also quite simple. These may have "wild" symbols, and may also have the multiplier symbols, and the cherries and bars and that's it.

On the other hand there are also several reel slot machines whose pay scales and play options have become very complex. These machines usually have a combination of wild, multiplier and scatter symbols, along with cherries, bars, numbers, 7s, colored 7s, and various near-jackpots, tertiary, secondary, and primary jackpots with various combinations of this-and-that, and so on. These may look interesting, but they can be hard to figure out. They are not necessarily bad machines to play, but they can be harder to understand. The harder they are to understand, the more time and thought you must commit before you make a financial investment in the game. Otherwise you are just tossing your money into the wind, hoping that some of it will land on a paying combination. That's not a very smart way to play slots. You should always *know* what the machine is, how it plays, and how it pays. You may choose to play it anyway, but at least you will have made that choice from an *informed opinion*.

The variety of pay situations becomes even more important for the newest video slots. On these games the varieties and options are so vast that it becomes even more crucial for you to *invest time to learn first*, and money to play only after that. Many of these games are so complex that most people simply don't know, or realize, what they have won, or how. That's bad. These players will not enjoy their gaming, and will likely lose a lot more money than necessary. As I mentioned above, these video slots usually provide quite extensive information in the "help" and "pay" menus, so look it up, read it, and *learn* before you play. A few minutes lost from your gambling time will mean a lot more gambling time in the end. You won't lose as much money, or as quickly, as you will if you play these games without knowing anything.

On these video slots, the variety of pays can often mean many very good opportunities for really good wins. Mostly, these multi-line multi-credit play machines will be nickels, with the possibility of wagering anywhere from the base one nickel per one payline, all the way to 250 coins on some machines for 20-line plays, or more. It all depends on the game, and the machine which supports this game. Some machines also offer multi-denominational games, and there you can actually select the value of your credits. You may be able to play for as little as one penny per credit to as much as $5 per credit, with the possibility of wagering anywhere from one credit to 45 credits, 90 credits, 100 credits, and even more per pull. Among these games the variety of symbols which activate various pays, bonuses, and options are so vast that it is crucial you investigate this before playing. Always look at the payoff display first, as well as all of the bonuses and scatters, and everything else which that machine, and that game, does.

In particular, look carefully to see if this game pays less than the play credits for the smallest pays. Many of these machines tend to give "deceiving" pays, because they aren't really pays at all. For example, many of these machines will cost you 45 coins to play, as maximum per pull, but the most frequent pay they will give you is only 36 coins. So, in effect, you are losing 9 coins each time you get this "pay." That's not a pay at all. It does, however, contribute to the longevity of your play since you won't be losing so much all the time, but the point is that you will be losing. Unless that machine's pay schedule offers a series of pays which can be hit relatively easily and in cumulative combinations with other pays, and these pays add up to significant amounts to overcome the losses on those more frequent "phantom pays," then this machine is only an entertainment console which will amuse you, but will eat your money. These are not among the best machines you can select, even though their variety of pays may include them in this "good" category.

It is difficult to identify what a "good" machine is, because many of these newest video games really aren't that good, while others are a lot better than just "good" would indicate. The best gauge I can offer you is the simplest: familiarity. If you are familiar with the machine's game, or concept, or theme (and here I am speaking specifically about the newest video slots), then you can make better judgments about the game and how it may affect your abilities to win. Also, if the game's variety of symbols seems confusing, it probably isn't the most viable candidate for your gaming investment, unless you are capable of performing the kind of research this game will require. This is called the game's "learning curve" and is often a problem for game designers. The question they often ask is: "How long will it take someone to learn this game and become sufficiently comfortable with it to invest their money and play it?" Well, that is largely subjective. Only you can answer that for yourself. I can give you guidelines, but the choice and decision and ability to follow these guidelines must be your own.

So for reel slots, look for a variety of symbols, pays, and bonuses which are easily identified and understood. For video games, look for familiar themes, or games, and always invest the learning time first, by reading the pay information, bonus information, and help screens before you invest your money. Following these simple tools will allow you to find the best variety of options on the slots, as well as the best investment for your gaming dollars.

Frequent Pays

Among reel slots, this means a machine which will hit at least the very minimum pay once about each four pulls, on average. This may seem aggressive, but if you keep count of how many spins you make before you get a pay, what this pay amount was, and how many spins before the next pay, and what *that* amount was, and so on, you will come to an average of a pay once about each 3.4 pulls, for an average pay of 6.8 coins (for 2-coin reel slots). I have played tens of thousands of pulls on such machines. When I was working as a consultant to the casino industry, part of my task was to research slot machines, players' habits, machine pays, and so on. During these years I have accumulated data from hundreds of thousands of slot players and millions of slot pulls. On the 2-coin reel slots, which are the only reel slots

I recommend you play, the machines I call "good" fall into the category of the mean (average) minimum pays. It doesn't seem like much, and it certainly has nothing to do with the machine's overall payback percentage. This is merely an observational estimate based on real-world experiences.

To understand what this means is not very hard. On average, you should get a hit of at least triple your maximum-coin-per-pull investment (2 coins for these reel machines) once every four spins. This is an average pay of at least 6 coins in four pulls. This is a net loss to you of about 2 coins, because the four pulls cost you 8 coins, while your average return is about 6 coins. These are figures rounded off for ease of example. In reality, this will not happen just exactly this way. As I've stated, these are averages over many events. What will happen in reality on these machines is that you should hit your minimum pay on the machine's pay display at least once each 8 coins invested, and this pay should be at least twice the amount of your maximum-coin play. For example, if you are playing a $1 reel slot machine where the maximum coins are 2 ($2 per pull), then you should hit at least a $4 pay once every four spins. If you do, then this is one of the better machines and therefore falls into this category of "good."

On most of these machines you will find that they pay these minimum pays more often, but the example above should serve as a guideline for the majority of such machines. The key to look for is the *amounts* of these minimum pays. For the maximum-coin play of 2 coins, the *minimum pay* on these machines must be at least 4 coins. If it is, this is the machine which I recommend. If it does not have this minimum pay structure, then you will have to weigh other factors to decide if this machine should be a candidate for your gaming investment. It may still be a viable machine to play, based upon the remaining majority of factors I am listing in my Top-10 list. Just because the machine doesn't have this one aspect doesn't necessarily disqualify it entirely. There are quite a few machines which will more than offset this minimum-pay requirement by the various other options they offer, making them an equally good investment because of the variety, size, and frequency of their other pays. As a good rule of thumb, however, taking advantage of the research I have done and recognizing the kinds of machines and their pays I have indicated will provide you with a very good gauge to find the most liberal and best-paying reel machines now available on the casino floor.

Graduated Pay Scale

Although I generally don't like the *traditional* buy-a-pay machines, I am pleased to report that most of those old teasers are gone from the slot floor. These were machines that offered pays only on single bars for 1 coin, then double bars for 2 coins, and then the 7s and jackpots only on 3 coins bet. These are deadly, and aren't around much anymore. However, just because these old machines had a bad reputation doesn't mean that all buy-a-pay machines are bad. Among reel slots, machines that offer a graduated pay scale which also pays more money for the top two, or even three, jackpots for the maximum-coin play are actually among the very best kinds you can find.

For example, you may find reel slots which offer doublers, or triple-pay multiplier symbols, where the top jackpot (usually all three of the multiplier symbols lined up) pays $1,000 for the jackpot with 1-coin play, but pays $2,500 for the same hit with 2-coin play. Other machines may offer a similar differential. For example, some machines offer a $4,000 pay for the 1-coin hit, but a $10,000 jackpot for the 2-coin hit. Others offer a $1,500 jackpot for the 1-coin hit, but $4,000 for the 2-coin hit on the same jackpot combination. These are all technically buy-a-pay machines, because you "buy" the pay for the top jackpot extra-money award when you wager that extra second coin (or third coin, or fifth coin, or whatever number of coins is required to hit the top jackpot).

You don't have to be a financial genius to understand that *the advantage lies entirely in wagering the maximum coin.* And since I am speaking of reel slots right now, and since I am advising you to seek out and play only the 2-coin machines, then it is pretty clear that the investment of that extra $1 is well worth it. If you don't play that second coin on these machines, or that maximum-coin wager (whatever the maximum may be on that machine), then you are not getting the best payoff percentage of which that machine is capable. Many of these machines are among the most liberal reel slots you are ever likely to find. Many are 98 percent payback machines, and some are even 99 percent payback machines but—and this is a very big "but"—this payback percentage is very largely vested in that extra money you get when you hit the top jackpot with the 2-coin bet. Otherwise, the single-coin wager payback is very much lower, and can be as low as 80 percent. The point is that these buy-a-pay machines are very good payers, but you must play that $2 per pull, or you will not get the money, or the payback percentage, to which you would otherwise be entitled.

Many people habitually play only 1-coin in these machines (and others like them) without realizing that they aren't saving any money but are instead cheating themselves out of the good pays which they would be getting for the correct 2-coin play. They are also substantially lowering their payback percentage, because their miserly play doesn't take advantage of the liberal payback program which these machines have—for the correct maximum-coin wager. These people give large amounts of their wins back to the casino, because they don't force the casino to pay them the correct amount for their wins, to which they are entitled.

They are ignorant of the fact that they are perennial losers only because they are so miserly they play badly even on good machines. Don't do this. If you go to a casino to play a slot machine, don't waste your money and don't try to "save" money by silly plays like this. You're not saving anything, you're simply making yourself an even bigger loser, and a sure loser at that. That's why casinos can offer so many of these well-paying machines: because many of their players will play them badly, and as a direct result, the casino rakes in the money.

This situation applies only to the reel slots, and only to these reel slots which offer bigger pays for the top of the graduated pay scale for the maximum-coin play. There are other machines which may look identical to these buy-a-pay machines, but which only double the payoff for each extra coin wagered. These are the "doublers" as opposed to the buy-a-pays. To continue with the 2-coin-maximum wager examples, these are machines which will pay double the 1-coin wager amount for the second-coin wager, but will not pay anything "extra," like the buy-a-pays. For example, this kind of machine may pay $1,000 for the jackpot for a 1-coin wager, $2,000 for the same jackpot for the 2-coin wager, and double the amount for all other pays for the second-coin wager. While the buy-a-pay machines usually also pay double only for the graduated scale of smaller pays for the second-coin wager, those machines will pay you that "extra" money for the top jackpot, or even the top two or three jackpots, for the 2-coin wager. That's why they are the "buy-a-pay" machines. The doublers will not do this. These machines just double every pay for each extra coin played. This also applies to such machines which may be 3-coin machines, or even 5-coin machines or more. Some of the video slots are of this kind, the doublers, where for each additional coin wagered you not only activate another payline, but can also double your pay for that payline by wagering that extra coin, or coins, for as many coins as the machine allows for as many paylines as it may have. Although this is also similar to the buy-a-pay principle, they are more closely related to the doublers. It's kind of a combination of a doubler and a buy-a-pay machine, because some of these will also pay extra for the maximum-coin wagers. (More on this when we discuss video slots.)

For reel slots, this is evident in the simplicity of the pay scale. Most of these doubler reel slots will be in the 2-coin and 3-coin versions. Many will look exactly like the more lucrative buy-a-pay machines but will not pay you anything more for your maximum-coin wagers. For this reason, these kinds of machines, and *only* these kinds of reel slots, are a candidate for single-coin play. The reason is obvious: You are not getting anything extra for the second coin wager, and therefore the machine's payback percentage remains the same no matter how many coins you wager. The decision is then up to you, whether you want to double your pays by wagering the 2 coins, or whether you simply want to last longer, gain the same payback percentage, and simply play 1 coin per pull. But be very careful! Do not confuse these machines with the buy-a-pays, or with progressives, or any other kind of machine that pays something extra for the maximum coin wager. These doubler machines are very lucrative as an investment, either because of their inherently liberal payback program, or because you can still gain their maximum payback with only 1-coin bets. But if you confuse them with the other kinds, then you may be shooting yourself in the foot, and costing yourself money. Make sure that the machine you are about to play is either the doubler or the buy-a-pay. If all the pays are merely doubled for that extra coin, then this is a doubler. If the machine offers the top jackpot, or the top two or three jackpots, with extra pays for the second-coin wager, then this is the buy-a-pay machine and you *must* wager that extra coin (or coins) to take advantage of its payback percentage and maximize your winning opportunities.

Both of these kinds of machines are what I call "good." It just depends on how you want to play them. Always play the maximum coins in any machine, unless it's merely a doubler. Then decide whether you want to invest the second coin for double-the-pay, or just play it 1 coin at a time. On the reel slot doublers, this is a good way to play. On the video slots, however, this is never a good option. On all buy-a-pay reel slots, which include all of the bonus slots, progressives, and extra-jackpot reel slots, and on most of the *newest* video slots, never play only one coin. On these machines you must always play maximum coins to get the best pays to which you are entitled by the machine's program. The only exception is video slots where the wagering of maximum coins does not factor in the pays you will be able to receive. Such machines are the kinds where the top jackpot is awarded on any payline, and pays only double the relative amount per-coin wagers. These kinds of video slots are rare. Most of the video slots you will play will always pay more for the maximum-coin wager. Most of them, and I am pretty sure that 99 percent of all such video slots fall into this category, will pay you the maximum award only if you play the maximum coins. Therefore, as I have already mentioned, it is ever more important that you take the time to see what the machine pays, how much, when, on which combination, and what the coin-in requirements are.

Multipliers That Substitute

Multipliers are those symbols that multiply the pay, such as "double" or "triple" symbols, or whatever-the-amount-to-multiply-symbols they may be. When these also substitute for all the other symbols on the game, this makes that machine among the very best you can find. There are, however, subtle differences among the kinds of machines which employ these various symbols. Although many of these machines may look identical, they may not in fact be the same game or offer the same payoffs. For example, many machines offer either the double or the triple symbol multipliers, showing these in circular configuration. Other machines are absolutely identical to these machines with the multiplier symbols, but on these machines the symbols are merely "wild". This means that they substitute for all the other symbols, or at least for the majority of the other symbols, but do not multiply the pays. These symbols are also configured in a circular picture, and this may even look almost identical to the other kinds of symbols which are the multiplier. But on these symbols, if you look carefully, it says "wild." You must be very careful to see all these little tricks which can be found on many reel slots. These multipliers may not actually substitute for the other symbols, or may substitute only for some symbols, or may factor only when hit in combinations with other specific symbol hits. All of this can get pretty confusing. The simplest rule that I can give you to help you overcome this confusion is to look at the payoff display on the reel slot machine you are thinking of playing. If the payoff display shows a lot of various and confusing symbols, and other kinds of combinations, then this is one of those machines where not all symbols will be multipliers, not all symbols will substitute for other symbols, and not all symbols may be wild. Also, on such machines it is quite likely that you will have to hit very specifically detailed combinations of various symbols before you get any pays, and certainly before you get any kind of jackpot pays. These machines are not your best investment. The more stuff they show, the harder it is to hit. Your best choices can be found among the simplest of the reel slots. These are those machines that show simple pays, either as doublers, or as the graduated pay scale I mentioned earlier. These machines may have double, or triple, symbols, or even other many-more-times multipliers, but they will have a relatively simple display showing the pays. These are by far your best choice. The simpler the machine, usually, the better the pays.

Among reel slots, the best overall machines are those that have a multiplier symbol which also substitutes for all other symbols. On some machines, very rare these days, such symbols may also pay as a scatter. Generally, though, you will be quite likely to find 2-coin-maximum reel slots with multiplier symbols which also substitute for others. When you find a machine where these multipliers also substitute for all other symbols, you've got one of the best machines currently available. Be careful to note whether these symbols are stated as "matching" other symbols. A symbol which is a "match" for other symbols does not necessarily substitute for all *combinations* of symbols. Such a symbol is a "match" only if hit in combination with other like symbols which would have constituted that specific paying combination. This is normally found on the newest multi-line video machines, where many symbols are shown as "match" symbols for some other specified symbol or series of symbols. But being a "match" doesn't mean that these substitute. There's a big difference. Substitute symbols will make a win no matter what other symbols are showing, because the substitute symbol will also substitute for the smallest pay and, therefore, will make you a win even if hit all by itself in that position on the reels. A "match" symbol will not do this. It will pay only if it is hit with other like symbols, and therefore now this combination forms a winning "match." On these video slot machines, such problems with "match" symbols are somewhat offset by the fact that most of these machines also include multiplier and scatter symbols as well as these "match" symbols. This allows for a sufficient variety of winning combinations to overcome the detrimental effect of separating the "match" symbols from substituting multipliers.

On reel slots, these "match" symbols are less common, but they can still be found on some machines, particularly on machines with many different combinations of possible wins. This is very apparent on machines which use a multitude of various symbols, such as double, triple, wild, and match symbols all at once, or in various combinations. There are enough of these machines on the casino floor to warrant this warning. *Stay away from them, because they will more than likely eat up your bankroll.* Concentrate rather on the far more lucrative simpler machines I described earlier, and try to look for machines that have the combination of bonus + substitute + multiplier, where all these functions are performed by the same symbol. These will be the better games for you among the reel slots.

Generous Bonus Structure

Many reel slot machines will offer you what seem like huge and easy-to-hit bonus pays. The simple truth is that the more bonuses there are, and the more they appear to pay, the harder they are to hit. The casino operators love these games; even if a player wins, in reality he has lost and the casino has won. To be sure, these machines have some of the highest casino "hold" percentages of any slots. This doesn't mean that they aren't fun to play, but as a smart slot player you should be aware of the realities behind these kinds of machines, and the very long odds of getting suitable wins on them. Remember, when you consider playing any of these machines, or any "bonus" type reel slot machine, that the "special" or "bonus" features *are an illusion.* Whatever the winning event may be is preprogrammed into the machine's play chip, and therefore that "bonus" event is actually not a random event but a predetermined one. The "costs" of these player wins which the machine pays out (and hence the casino pays out) are already factored in the machine's program, and therefore you are not getting something extra, but are in fact getting what you would have gotten anyway had the machine simply paid that amount more on the reel-slot pay itself. Of course if you happen to be the lucky player who hits the top jackpot, you cash in big time. The best advice I can give you for any casino gaming investment, and for profitable slot play in the long run, is not to invest the *majority* of your gaming money into these "bonus" reel slot machines. Try it for $20, or $100, or so, but if you don't hit a decent pay on this investment, save the rest of your money and go play the many other better-paying machines which are available all over the casino.

There are, of course, other kinds of "bonus" machines that offer an entirely different pay structure to these kinds of bonus games. Many of these machines will feature bonuses which can be achieved by extra-coin plays. These are a version of the buy-a-pay machine, and are often called "buy-a-bonus" machines. Although they are mostly among the video slots these days, there are some reel slots which can be classified in this subcategory. What differentiates the generous bonus structure from the run-of-the-mill bonus games is the fact that these bonuses are reasonable, and reasonably achievable. Even though these bonuses, particularly on reel slots, are really all part of the overall preprogrammed payback percentage of that machine or game, that program actually allows for the *frequent* occurrence of these events, sufficiently so that the pays thus received contribute significantly to the overall generally liberal nature of the game itself. This won't mean much to you if you don't know how to find these machines which can be hard to do, but there are some key factors to seek out: Look for bonus machines that offer stepped or tiered bonuses with at least triple-the-amount hierarchy between each step up the bonus structure. For example, if the smallest bonus is 10 coins, the next highest should be at least 30 coins, the next highest at least 90 coins, and so on, or as close to this scale as you can find it. Then, at least the top three bonuses should be 500 coins and more from that point on, and up. Finally, the hierarchy should not exceed more than ten steps up the bonus structure. Any more than that, and it will be too hard to hit the better pays. Any less than that, and the pays may not be worth enough to warrant the play. Of course, this depends on the game itself. On some games, the hierarchy may only be a few steps, but it will have a high hit frequency. This is very often the case especially with the video slots. On other games, the hierarchy may be extended, and the top pays very large indeed, such as even $1 million, and perhaps more. There are many reel slots with similar structures, while there are some video slots which also use this extended bonus hierarchy, although in video slots this usually means second- and third-screen bonuses.

The best way to gauge whether this machine belongs in this category of "good" machines, and under this sub category of generous bonus structure which actually hits often enough to warrant play, is to look for the simplest series of three-times-graduated scale for the reel slots or to look for multiple bonuses and second- and third-screen bonus features on the video slots. Of course, this is in addition to the other factors listed in my Top 10.

Sizable Pays and Frequent Scatters

Sizable pays fall into two subcategories. First, for reel slots, it means that the smallest pays are at least twice the amount of the maximum-coin wager. Second, for reel slots, it means that the top jackpot, and preferably the top two or three jackpots, offer higher pays for the maximum-coin wager, over and above merely paying a multiple of the base double, such as in the doubler machines. Of course, this also combines with some of the other preferred principles of my Top-10 list. This is particularly important for reel slots which have multipliers which also substitute for all other symbols, or perhaps pay the minimum pay when showing up on the reel by themselves. For example, such a reel slot machine may offer a 4-coin pay for a hit of a single cherry (2-coin wager), and will also pay this when the multiplier symbol lands on the payline all by itself, or with another combination (other than cherries) which normally would not pay a win. This machine most definitely qualifies as "good" under my general category, specifically for these two reasons (plus any other positive features it may have, of course). On other machines similar to this one, there may not be any cherries, but the multiplier symbol or symbols themselves may pay the minimum pay when only one of them hits on the payline in a combination which doesn't make any higher pay. These machines are also of this preferred kind.

The situation of frequent scatters applies mostly to the video slots. The vast majority of the newest video slots offer not only a multitude of pays, and many paylines and bonuses, but also one or more "scatter pay" features as well. Such scatter pays are additional bonuses that offer pays when these symbols show anywhere in the window whether or not they are aligned on any payline. Most will pay a graduated scale of pays, depending on the number of coins wagered and the number of paylines activated. As in some of the reel slots, many of these video slot bonuses depend largely on the maximum-coin wagers to offer the best and biggest rewards. This also applies to scatters, because on some of these games you may not be able to get these scatter pays, or at least take full advantage of the bonus pays they offer, if you either do not play all the paylines or, which is more common, don't wager the maximum-coin bet. Nevertheless, almost all of these video slots will pay you at least something for a scatter pay under most circumstances, even if you wager the minimum number of coins, as long as (on most machines) you wager at least one coin per available payline. This means at least the minimum bet of 9 coins for a 9-line machine, 12 coins for a 12-line machine, 20 coins for a 20-line machine, and so on. Although doing this may not reward you with the most money these machines are set to pay on such hits, it should pay you at least something.

The frequency of these scatter hits is one of the key indicators of how good this video machine may be. There are several other indicators, such as many of the items I have listed in this chapter. The scatter pays, however, offer the best "window" into the machine's overall program. There are some machines which offer very attractive scatter pays, but when you play these games you will hardly ever hit any of them and this therefore makes the scatters all but useless. Many such scatters offer even second-screen and third-screen extra bonuses, and award additional games, or plays, or even launch you into an entirely new game. Beware of such offers. As I have stated earlier, the more stuff there is, the harder it is to get, and the more it will cost you, not only on the base game, which has to collect enough money to make these bonuses available, but also because the bonuses themselves are often very disappointing. On many such machines these scatters may tout such lucrative wins, but to get them you must hit at least four of the scatter symbols, or hit all five, or hit them on specific reels, such as only on the first three, the middle three, the last three, or hit them only adjacent to each other, and so on and on. All these "restrictions" make these scatter pays all but invalidate any such wins which you might hit. Also, many times you will get a hit of these scatters, but will only hit the minimum, be it two or three, or whatever the number for a "minimum" scatter hit may be. Then you will only get a very small pay, such as 50 coins for example, while it cost you 45 coins to hit it. So you made a profit of a mere 5 coins. Well, add up all the coins which you had invested in the time it took you to hit this scatter pay, and you will soon discover that the machine has actually cost you $100 or more, and all you got was a mere 5 coins.

This example may not be applicable to all such machines, but it is indicative of the kind of frequency, and the kind of regular pays, which you will encounter on many of these machines. You should therefore investigate the structure of such scatter pays and make a determination on the likelihood of such hits actually having a positive effect on your win expectation. If it looks too good to be true, it usually is. Therefore, I would encourage you to look for machines with very *simple* scatter pay options—scatters you can easily identify, and pays you can easily quantify. For example, there are several machines which use gold coins as the scatter symbol. On many of these machines—such as my personal favorite, called *Double Bucks*™—any two of these coins will immediately pay you double your base-wager bet. This is the same principle as with the reel slots, where the minimum pay is equal to twice the maximum-coin wager. If you find a scatter pay scale on your machine where the minimum required hit is merely two of the scatters, and they pay double the base-wager bet amount, then you have found one of the most liberal video slots around.

Be wary, however, of machines which only look like the ones I am describing, but have other features which are linked in some way to the scatter events. These machines may offer the gold coins symbols, but they work only on some reels, and not on others. There are machines, for example, where these scatter symbols are only on the first, third, and fifth reels. These are most definitely *not* among the better machines you can find.

In general, seek out video slots which offer simple scatter

pays with simple pay structures and no other "extra" bonuses, such as entry into other rounds or screens (referring
here, of course, only to the scatters, and not to the bonuses
which enter you into the "bonus screens"). The simpler the
scatter pay, the more it will pay and the more often it will
hit. Ultimately, you will have to do some field trials of the
machine you select. On a 45-coin nickel machine, take a $40
investment. Playing maximum coins, if you hit the minimum scatter pays at least four times during your 800-coin
play, then this is one of the better-paying video slots. Combine your valuations of this machine with the other features
of this Top-10 list, and the other comments, observations,
and suggestions in this book, and you will be empowered
with the best knowledge available for your slot machine decisions, as these apply to these specified video slots.

Minimum 94 Percent Payback

Most people don't know that almost all of the states that
offer legalized gambling publish the slot payback percentages on a monthly basis. You can easily obtain these figures
by writing either to *Midwest Gaming and Travel* magazine
or to the Gaming Regulatory Board, or Agency, in your state.
If the state gaming legislation requires that these figures be
published, which is the case for most states, you will be able
to actually see which kinds of slots paid what, how much,
and at what average payback percentage. This is very helpful in selecting not only where you will play, but also which
kinds of slot machine you should try. As you see this information, you will quickly discover that the nickel machines
are the worst (other than some of the better video slots), that
the quarter machines aren't much better, and that the best
payback percentages, on the average, are found among $1
and $5 reel slots. Of course, the $25 and higher "high-

roller" slots also offer many of the better paybacks, but most people can't afford to play these kinds of machines.

You should note, however, that often this information will not provide you with details or specifics about individual machines or casinos. The information is merely general, and will show you that in your state, the $1 and $5 machines, all counted together, paid an average of this-many-percent (whatever that figure may be). And so on for all the other kinds of machines which your state permits in legalized casinos. Therefore, you will only find out the average payback statewide, and not the specific payback per casino, and certainly not per machine. Nevertheless, this is still a very good indicator of the overall general status of your kind of slot machine in that state. If, for example, you see that the majority of the $1 and $5 reel slot machines in your state pay merely an average of, say, 91.2 percent, then you know that it will be far better for you to take a trip elsewhere, even if you have to invest in a drive or a plane ticket. If you still go and play these machines in that state, then you will know that your trip is likely to cost you more than it would have had you invested in a plane ticket and hotel rooms somewhere else, because these machines are such bad payers that you will lose a lot, and more often. Remember that these are averages, and that therefore many machines will be paying back even less than these meager paybacks.

As a general rule, the casinos in Nevada have the best reel slot payback percentages of any state in the United States, and much better than most of the tribal casinos. Tribal casinos are sovereign nations, and therefore are not required to report their slot machine paybacks as a general rule. Some do, voluntarily, and some may be required to do so, but most do not.

In southern Nevada, particularly in Las Vegas, most of the reel slot machines on the Strip and Downtown will be set at an average of at least 94.7 percent payback. Many will actually pay back 98 percent, and be so identified and so set and no "up to" statements included. Northern Nevada, and some of the more regional centers in other Nevada cities, will have somewhat lower payback percentages as an *average*, with paybacks of around 92 percent to 94 percent. However, even in these gaming cities there are casinos which offer many of the better-paying reel slots, and so this is, again, merely the average. If you are smart enough to know what to look for, you can find these better reel slots even in regions where the general average payback is considerably lower than what you should look for before you invest your gaming dollar.

For video slots, the situation is somewhat different. Because most of the video slots are classified as "nickels," their statistics are included in the "nickels report" part of the payback percentage statements offered by those states which publish this information. In addition, these figures also include other video games, such as video poker, video keno, and video blackjack, and this further confuses the final figures. Here we are considering only the reel slots, which in this instance happen to be video slots. This book has nothing to do with video poker (for a discussion of video poker, I refer you to my book *Powerful Profits from Video Poker*).

Determining the average payback on video slots is challenging, but not insurmountable. Eliminating the video poker machines in the nickel denomination, and the other video games in nickel denominations, will leave us with about a 20 percent to 30 percent fluctuation. This is a very large discrepancy, but we are only interested in a percentage payback *average* guide here, and not with hard-and-fast figures. In addition, you also have to take into account the fact that most of these video slots take 45 coins to play, with many taking 90 coins and even more. Therefore, although they are listed in these reports as "nickels," they actually are nothing of the sort. They are either $2+ machines, or near-$5 machines, or are even more costly. Definitely not "nickels" as traditionally understood.

Factoring this information and the percentage differential into the stated payback percentages, and doing some educated guesswork, you can arrive at a reasonable assumption of the actual nickel payback percentage for video slots. This will lead you to discover that the average, in most states, is around 75 percent to 80 percent payback. This is almost as bad as for live keno, the worst game for payback odds. No wonder the casinos love these video slots. Your wallet can dry up very quickly playing such machines. But this is not always so. Many *video* slots offer much better payback percentages. Overall, however, the old-style nickel *reel* slot machines are generally among the worst paying of all the machines found on the casino floor.

I will qualify this somewhat by restating that quite a number of the *newest video slots* can actually be played to better paybacks than these overall statistics indicate. This is because by wagering the maximum coins, you can often "buy-a-pay" which makes the game pay back much closer to the 94 percent, and even as high as 98 percent, a payback most often associated with the high-roller slots. That's because many of these machines have payback programs which *reward* maximum-coin play! Even if this machine doesn't have such features, the very act of forcing the game to pay you back the maximum it allows provides you with the better pay opportunities. More on these nickel slots a little later. For now, remember that the nickel *reel* slots are in general the worst-paying games available on the casino floor. However—and this is very important—please do not confuse these old-style nickel *reel* slots with some of the *newest video slots*, which happen to have a 5¢ (nickel) base coin-unit-value. Many of these new video slot machines can indeed be played to *much better payback percentages* than such averages (as stated for all of the "nickel" slots) may indicate from among the averages in such slot payback percentage reports. To determine which are the better games, follow the information listed in this Top-10 list, the suggestions listed elsewhere in this book, and, in particular, those machines which I describe in Part Two.

Ticket Printers sans Coins

If you're playing reel slots, particularly the $1 or $5 machines, most of the time you won't have many problems with the coins, coin hoppers, or coin fills. On these reel slots, if you hit a high-paying combination, this is normally paid by hand by the attendant. Sometimes, however, you will have to cash out accumulated coins. When this happens, and you have 200 coins or more, then you will have two main problems. First, where to put them. Casinos used to offer racks for coins, but this is no longer so in most casinos. Now you will see plastic buckets. These are okay, but many casinos have only buckets that are much too small for the coins that customers will actually put in them. This will mean that you will have to fill up several of these buckets with your slot wins and then carry them to the nearest change booth, which is often not very near or easily found, or easily accessible, or actually open. If you finally do find a booth, and are strong enough to haul these heavy coins over there, and don't spill your buckets along the way, good luck to you. If that's the case, this usually means that you have also had to wait for a hopper fill. Most of these machines are designed to carry up to $400 worth of coins, and that's it. Therefore, if you have won several non-jackpot pays in a row, or over time, and are now ready to cash them out, chances are that your machine has run out of coins. Now the light will flash. Relax, because in most casinos it will take at least fifteen minutes before any of the employees actually responds to your machine's signal for attention. This is usually due to the fact that casinos grossly understaff their slot floors, and therefore all the people there are so busy they simply can't get to you any sooner. Of course, in some casinos these annoying delays will also be due to the fact that the employees may be far too busy talking to each other in some remote corner of the casino, blissfully ignorant of the fact that your machine needs service. Both of these situations are painfully obvious to everyone—except the casino management, or so it seems.

So now you have to wait. Once the attendant arrives, he will have to open the machine, look inside, rummage around, write some details on a paper log inside, send a computer signal, close the machine, go to the computer, print out the fill request ticket, go to the change booth, wait for the person to become available, get the bag with the coins, carry it back to your machine, insert their authorization card into the machine's card reader, punch more codes, call at least one other person, possibly two, wait for them to show up, then when they do show up the attendant with the fill bag has to open the machine again, cut the cord on the bag of coins, dump the coins in the hopper, wait for all these other people to sign the fill slip, then close the door, and punch some more codes into the computer. Then, if you're lucky, the machine will pay you out the rest of your coins. Unless, that is, you have accumulated more credits than the machine can hold coins for in any one fill, in which case it will run empty again, and you will now have to go through this entire procedure one more time. I don't know how you feel, but this annoys me no end.

This situation is even more problematic for quarter and nickel machines, especially the nickel video slot games, which take 45 coins, or 90 coins, or more, as maximum bets per pull. On these machines you can accumulate credit very quickly. The most annoying feature of these games is that they will pay out anywhere up to 1,500 coins from the hopper. Anything over those amounts is, usually, a hand pay, so this situation becomes easier. Say that you are playing at a machine such as this, and you have 975 credits, and you want to leave. You press the cash-out button (or video icon), and now the machine starts to spill out these 975 coins. Unfortunately, most of these machines have very small cash-out coin drop trays. On the slant-top machines, these drop trays are merely narrow deep holes on the right-hand side of the machine. This makes the act of collecting all these tiny coins an exercise in complete frustration. Not only will it take "forever" (at least ten minutes) for this amount of coins—and a lot longer if you need fills or experience coin jams (which happens a lot)—but you will also get your hands and arms extremely dirty. Then you will have to stuff all these coins into tiny buckets, haul those to the one change booth which is actually open, and wait there until it's your turn, all the while trying to balance these buckets full of your nickels, and all for a pay of a little less than $50. It's just insane, but casinos still insist on this idiocy.

Fortunately, more and more games are available with ticket printers instead of coin hoppers. Some of these machines even have a combination of ticket printers and coin hoppers. Since some players still like the thrill of hearing their tiny coins hitting the collection tray, these machines will pay you out coins for small pays, usually up to about $10 worth of coins. Any pay larger than this, and the machine will print you a ticket instead. Many of these tickets are bar-coded so that they can easily be cashed at any change booth or the casino cashier. Also, many of these tickets can actually be used as same-as-cash for play in other machines. Simply stick this ticket into the machine's bill acceptor; it will scan the bar code and credit that amount of money to your credit meter. Same as using cash. This makes life a whole lot easier for everybody. The casino doesn't have to carry that many small coins, such as nickels and quarters, you don't have to wait for coin fills, or wait for coin jam repair, and you don't have to wait around forever for those annoying small jackpot pays.

Although these games are actually $1 games, and even $5 games, when you wager the maximum coins, they are still set to lock up for any jackpot of 1,000 coins or more. When you are playing 45 coins, or 90 coins or more, pays in excess of 1,000 coins are quite common. So every time you hit one of these average pays, these silly machines will lock up, and now you have to sit around for half an hour waiting for someone to bring you $50 cash, when that equates to merely a few pulls. These machines should be set for open-ended credits, so that each of these wins simply adds up on your credit meter, and when you are ready to cash out, it should then lock up only for a hand pay, or just give you the ticket instead. Casino management knows this, but they continue to ignore it, causing themselves financial losses during the "dead" time the machine is sitting idle while you are waiting for your money, and causing you, their customer, anxiety and frustration.

To be fair, there are many casino executives who have seen this problem and have corrected it by ordering the newest crop of video machines which not only carry these ticket printers, along with some hopper coin pays, but also contain the open-credit meter options, so that customers don't always have to wait for meaningless hand pays when all they do is hit a minor pay with a large per-pull and per-line wager. This too will improve with time. Therefore, whenever possible, look for machines which print tickets instead of drop coins such as ones I describe in the next section. This will save you time, keep your hands clean, and provide you with better enjoyment in the casino.

I also mentioned the location of the machine itself, its height and play buttons. There is now a whole new science in slot machine manufacture, called "cabinet ergonomics." This combines the cabinet design with the placement of the control buttons, bill acceptor, handle (if it still has one), club card reader, belly glass, and so on. This is only now becoming a concern to slot machine manufacturers, and has had little impact thus far on the casinos. While the manufacturer may take steps to see to it that the cabinet in which the machine is located is well made and not too high, the casinos habitually place these machines on cabinets which *are* too high. This is a relic from the older days, when the machines were short and the cabinets below hid the coin drop bucket where the casino's proceeds were dropped by the machine. Most of today's machines no longer do this, and if they do, the collection is small. Most of the casino's money is now in cash currency, fed by players into the bill acceptors.

Furthermore, many of these newest slot machines, reel slots in particular, are very tall and very large. (This also includes many of the video slots as well.) These large machines are then mounted on tall cabinets, which places the machine's controls so high you have to stand up, instead of sitting down, or reach up so high your arm gets tired very quickly. I don't like this; I don't think it's necessary in today's gaming environment. I think casinos should put these large machines at eye level *for a player who is sitting down*, not for a six-foot player standing up.

No Fixed Seats!

I also mentioned the fixed seating problem, common among many slant-top machines and some reel slots. These slot machines have seats in front of them which are fixed to the bottom of the machine's cabinet. Since these seats are not adjustable, they are usually mounted so far away from the game itself that you would have to be a six-foot-six-inch

300-pound man in order to fit there without having to sit at the very edge of the seat and have to bend over, and thus continually slip off the front of the seat while you are trying to reach the machine's controls and play the game. Although many casinos have done away with these kinds of seats, many still propagate this insanity, not only to their own financial detriment, but to the discomfort and bad backs of millions of their aching customers.

I would encourage you not to play any machine with a fixed seat mounted in front of it. When casinos see more and more players avoiding these silly seating arrangements, and start to realize that these machines aren't making any money for them because players aren't playing them, then the casinos will take those seats away and replace them with the free-standing armchair-style seats which are now common in many casinos.

In this last of the Top-10 list, I also mentioned the possible 10(a) category of small coin trays, or dark, tiny, coin drop holes on the slant-top machines. Many of these older machines have coin trays so tiny that you simply cannot get your hand in there, take a palmful of coins, and then be able to take your hand out again without having to open the palm and drop the coins right back. If you do get your fist out, you will most likely skin your knuckles. If you can't get it out, then you have to scoop up the coins with your fingers. For women, this is a very special problem. With every scoop of the coins from these tiny trays, they risk breaking their nails. This also applies to men, especially since many of these trays are made so badly that they loosen up with constant abuse, and often the rivets snap, revealing very sharp corners. I have cut my hands, fingers, and knuckles on these machines so many hundreds of times that I now buy several packs of Band-Aids at a time, and always carry at least ten of them in my pockets every time I go to the casinos to play machines. It is a very big problem, largely ignored by the casinos and slot machine manufacturers.

This is, however, changing. As slots evolve, soon they will pay out only in tickets, or credits credited to a credit-card-like card carried by all slot players. This is already happening. The ticket printers are one step toward this new world, called "coin-free" gaming. The other option is where no cash is used at all, but instead all play is done from that credit-card-like card. This is called "cashless gaming." Eventually, all machines will be cashless, or at least coin-free.

For now, when you select your machine, try the coin tray below. Put your hand inside, make a fist, and then try to get your hand out. If your hand hits the top lip of the machine, which hangs down over the coin tray, then this is a narrow coin tray and you will have to use your fingers to scoop up your coins, or risk skinning your knuckles. Although this should not necessarily disqualify this machine from the "good" category, it should at least be noticed. It is just one more of these items which, together, make up what I call the "good" slot machines.

THE BAD AND THE UGLY

Ah, so we are down to the last part of this chapter—the "bad" and the "ugly." What makes a "bad" slot machine? I guess that should be easy to answer: anything which does not possess the majority of all the Top-10 "good" features. Very rarely, in fact almost never, will you be able to find a slot machine which will have *all* of the "good" features I included in my list. Most of the time you will have to weigh all these factors, and find out how many of these features the machine actually possesses. If you get at least five out of the ten, then it's close. If you get more than five, you have found one of the best machines currently available.

What does this mean? To you, as a slot player, this means fewer losses, more time at the machine, more chances to score a win, more smaller wins along the way, longer time between dipping into your bankroll for more money, a more comfortable game and environment, and a better overall playing experience. Isn't that what your casino visit should be? Of course it should. It may take a little learning on your part, a little research, a little discipline, but in the end it will provide you with the ability to exercise your powers of choice. Remember that you have all the choices. You don't have to play a certain machine. You don't even have to play in that particular casino. You can choose. With this information, you can choose more wisely.

Finally, the "ugly." Well, that's a very relative term. The word "ugly" means different things to different people at different times. Its meaning is, therefore, transitory and cannot be significantly applied with any precision. To me, "ugly" means a lousy game, a machine which pays little or nothing, games which are too complex and confusing, bonuses which are so stretched that it's all but impossible to get them, hit them, or cash in on them with any kind of regularity or expected frequency. "Ugly" to me also means machines that look bad. They are too tall, too large, too hard to operate; they malfunction and are not repaired, have narrow trays or coin drop pits, have fixed seats, have that awful padding around the top, especially on slant-tops, where all sorts of grime and garbage accumulates. Games which are an obvious gimmick, or almost a downright scam. Big promises in pay schedule, without the delivery of equally viable hits and pays. "Ugly" in slot machines means to suck my money and not give me a fair payback. It means to have machines set at less than the minimum of 94 percent payback, for all kinds of machines, and not just the $1 and $5 games. It means little or no chance to get at least a good run for my investment.

As odd as this may sound, surveys indicate that the vast majority of people don't mind losing. Actually, they expect to lose. What they *do* mind, and significantly so, is to play games which eat their bankrolls, don't give them any play for their money, and thus no enjoyment at all, or very little, and with too frequent dips into the wallet or purse. As for me, I hate losing. I *always* expect to win. Without this in your mind, why play at all? If that is how you think about your slot play, I'd like to save you the trip money and the aggravation. Simply mail me your bankroll, and I will play it the way it should have been played—to win. I may not win, but darn it, I know I played it the best way it could be played, and in the best machines which can be found.

So finally, the really "ugly" means to waste money. It means not to play wisely, with knowledge, and with the absolute conviction and expectation that I can—and will—win, and that I am playing absolutely the best way possible. If you don't approach your slot play in this way, then you are part of the "ugly," and not the "good." This is so because no matter how much knowledge I can give you, in this book or any other, you won't do it that way; you do it *your* way. That is, of course, your right, but don't complain if you aren't satisfied with your casino experience, or mad that you lost. Honestly? I think that you are not that kind of a person, otherwise you would not have bought this book. So I end this chapter by wishing you the best, because that's where the "good" is really found.

Part Two

IGT: THE BIGGEST
AND THE BEST

Introduction

International Game Technology, known worldwide simply by the acronym IGT, is based in Reno, Nevada, and makes most of the games you will find in the casino. IGT is the biggest manufacturer of slot machines, slot progressives, and video slots in the world.

I have divided this part of the book into three chapters: chapter 4 focuses on traditional reel slot machines, chapter 5 on progressives, such as the popular *Megabucks*® and *Quartermania*™ machines, and chapter 6 on the great new video slot machines—many of which are already in the casinos—as well as some very new machines which will only start to appear on the casino floor in 2004.

These three chapters showcase the kinds of slot machines and games you will actually be playing when you visit your favorite casino. The IGT games are the standard by which all other slot machines are judged. IGT is by far the leader not only in the manufacture of slot machines, but also in the innovation of the games themselves. For example, it was IGT that introduced the first highly successful hybrid game, based on a popular theme. This was the *Wheel of Fortune*® machine. This game has spawned a number of other IGT games similar in style and format. The *I Dream of Jeannie*™ game, for instance, is a classic example of how designers were able to take the concept of the *Wheel of Fortune*® and adapt it to a video game hybrid which also uses a "bonus wheel," like the *Wheel of Fortune*® machine, but combined with a video slot machine game based on another popular television icon. These extremely popular and successful games can be found in every casino in the United States and in many casinos worldwide. They have become staples of casino gaming, and for that reason, I have decided to use them as a means of illustrating the present, and the future, of slot machines.

When you walk into any casino in the United States, you will immediately notice the vast expanse of the casino floor, largely occupied by slot machines. There are slots of every imaginable kind, from reel spinners to video slots, to progressives, bonus slots, and even more varieties of games and features within many of these games themselves. Most of these slots will be the ones you will read about here.

I have played IGT machines for many years, and much of my success as a slot player is due to the fact that I selected these games, my personal favorites among the crop of slots found in the casinos.

Reel Spinners

The term "reel spinner" simply refers to a traditional-style slot machine that employs spinning reels in the window display and has a handle to pull, as well as the now-common play buttons. Although these machines are now all computerized, they still retain the traditional style of the "mechanical" drums, with symbols that spin and come to a rest across the win-line shown on the front window of the machine. As I mentioned earlier, these were the kinds of machines which first spawned the revolution in slot machines.

Back in the old days, these were actual mechanical reels, activated by the pull on the handle and stopped by "stoppers" on the reels themselves. They were often hard to pull, and although genially called "one-armed bandits," these old machines were actually more commonly referred to as "the old clunkers." That was because they usually made a very distinct and loud clunking noise. Often the whole machine shook as these reels came to a stop. These old machines did not pay very much, or very often, and were highly susceptible to tampering and manipulation, or play by the use of slugs. For many years, however, they were the only available machines.

This is not so anymore.

Modern slot machines, like the ones I feature in this chapter, are well-made, computerized slots. They are smooth, they have comfortable controls, and they are completely tamper-proof. In fact, when you play one of these games on the casino floor, you can be completely assured that the game you are playing has been thoroughly tested and approved, and has been designed and maintained by IGT engineers to play to its optimum programmed potential. These are far from the old clunkers. Even though these still appear as the reel spinners of old, they are actually quite sophisticated games, using the latest technology to assure randomness as well as quality. This therefore means that you are getting a fair game which cannot be corrupted, and consequently you have the best chance to win.

Contrary to popular opinion, casinos and slot manufacturers do want you to win when you play their games. These games are designed to be entertaining, but they are also designed to *pay*. It's a common misconception among many people that slots are only designed to *take* your money. If that were true, no one would ever play them, because there would never be any winners. No winners, no customers. More winners means more publicity for the casino, and this means more *happy* customers.

I will now introduce you to some of the best games you will find in your favorite casino, as well as some games you may not yet have seen. Some of these descriptions will have an accompanying photo of the actual machine.

RED, WHITE & BLUE™

The first patriotically themed slot machine, this one is also the most popular. Originally configured as a 2-coin and a

3-coin slot machine, it featured the top jackpot when the red, white, and blue 7s were lined up correctly on the pay-line, in that precise order left to right. This game immediately caught the attention of slot players, not only because it had the most popular and easily recognizable themes, but also because it happened to pay very well. I have hit many jackpots on these machines; it's one of my personal favorites.

When these machines first appeared on the casino floor, they mostly were without any additional symbols. Just the various combinations of 7s, along with the traditional bars and cherries. Later, machines appeared with "wild" symbols on them, and then machines with "double" symbols. These features further enhanced the playing experience and also provided for some significant wins. One of the most common wins on this machine is the "mixed 7s" hit, a win where the various colored 7s appear on the win-line, but not in the jackpot configuration. On the 2-coin machine this usually paid 180 coins for maximum-coin play.

The newest of the very successful *Red, White & Blue*™ reel slots.

Now, with the addition of the double symbols, it has become possible to hit this quite frequent combination with the use of one or more of the double symbols. For example, if you hit the mixed 7s with just one of the double symbols, your mixed-7s pay would now be doubled. On these games, such a hit would commonly pay 360 coins instead of just 180. Of course, if you were lucky and hit two double symbols along with any 7, then you would have a double-double payoff, which would then combine with the payoff for the like-colored 7. For example, if you hit two double symbols with a red 7 showing on the second or third reel, you would now be paid for the winning combination of three red 7s, and this would be doubled and then doubled again. Hitting this combination with the red 7 on the first reel, then the double symbols, which also often substituted for all other symbols, would give you the top jackpot, because the other two symbols showing on reels 2 and 3 would then substitute for the white and the blue 7.

The newest version of this game is called the *Triple Double Red, White & Blue*™. This game features both the double-star and triple-star symbols, which combine not only to double, but also to triple the winning combinations when correctly lined up on the winning payline along with the other winning symbol, or symbols. Both symbols match any other symbol on the machine. One double-star doubles the payoff. Two double-stars pay four times the winning amount. One triple-star triples the pay, and two triple-stars pay nine times the winning amount. When one double-star and one triple-star show up, along with a winning symbol, then the pay is multiplied six times. Any combination of three star symbols wins the secondary jackpot, while the combination of all three triple-star symbols wins the top jackpot. This is one of the great games among reel spinners, and a game which can produce very lucrative wins.

TRIPLE LUCKY 7's™

This is the newest version of the *Lucky 7's*™ machines, which you have probably already played in your favorite casino. The most recent feature is the introduction of the "triple lucky 7's" symbol. This matches any other symbol on the game. When any one of these symbols lands on the payline with any other combination of winning symbols, the pay is tripled. And when two of the "triple lucky 7's" symbols appear on the payline with a matching winning symbol, then the pay is multiplied nine times. When all three of these symbols are correctly lined up on the payline, you win the top jackpot, based on the number of coins you played.

The latest of the *Triple Lucky 7's*™ reel slots.

This game features a variety of colored 7s, each paying in combinations with others, and more for hits when all like-colored 7s are achieved. The game can be found in 2-coin as well as 3-coin versions.

WILD THING™

Oh yes, even slot machines are getting racier! And none more so than this new gem, which features a luscious she-devil as one of the bonus symbols. It used to be that a machine called the *Wild Cherry*® was the most popular of the "wild" reel slots. Not anymore. Certainly not with this beauty looking at you.

This reel slot machine can be found in the 2-coin or 3-coin version. As with most of the machines in this section, it can also be found as a slant-top. This version of the game allows you to sit at the machine and look down on the window, which is mounted at a slight slant. It's designed to make you a little more comfortable, but it is still the same game as in the more traditional machines, which are often called "up-rights."

The lady devil on this game functions as a multi-plier when it lands on the payline with other winning symbols. And what a hit this is! When only one of these "wild things" hits with any other correctly achieved winning combination, the

That impish lady devil *Wild Thing*™ reel slot machine.

win is multiplied 12 times. Not to be outdone, the lady devil will make your bank account even richer when two of these symbols land on the payline with any other winning sym-bol. Now the win is multiplied 144 times! Now that's what I call a "wild thing."

Of course, if you land three of these symbols on the win-ning payline, you will win the top jackpot. Depending on the number of coins you wager, this jackpot can be quite large. On the 2-coin game, the top jackpot for the 2-coin wager is 20,000 coins, and even the 1-coin pay is 10,000 coins. It's sure to be one of the most popular reel slots you can find.

TRIPLE DOUBLE DOLLARS™

Many years ago one of the first "double" reel slot machines I played was called *Double Dollars™*. A terrific game for its day, it was the forerunner of all such similar slot machine games. It was also made by IGT, which pioneered the double and triple reel slots.

The *Triple Double Dollars™* reel slot.

This new game is based around that principle, and also based on the success of the series of double- and triple-dollars games which have been around for several years. These machines are also available in the 2-coin or 3-coin versions, and also either as an upright or a slant-top game. The double-dollars symbols match any other symbol on the game, and double the jackpot. Two of these symbols will pay four times the pay amount. The triple-dollars symbol also matches other symbols on the game, and pays triple the amount won with one symbol showing. If a triple and a double symbol combine for a win, then the pay is six times the amount shown on the payoff display. If two of the triple-dollars symbols are hit with a win, then this pay is multiplied nine times. Any combination of the mixed double and triple symbols will pay you the secondary jackpot, and the three triple-dollars symbols correctly appearing on the payline will pay the top jackpot. As always, the amount of such a jackpot depends on how many coins you wagered.

12 TIMES PAY™

This is the latest in a series of reel slots based around the popular double-dollars and triple-dollars games. First there were the *Five Times Pay*™ machines. You have probably played these, as they are quite popular and available in every casino. Then there were the *Ten Times Pay*™ machines, the next step up from the fives. Now this new game, the *12 Times Pay*™ machine, further explores the winning possibilities first introduced in the other kinds of machines, similar to this one.

In this new game, the special *12 Times Pay*™ symbol matches any other symbol, and will pay you 12 times the winning combination if only one of them is so hit along with the normal winning combination. When two of these symbols are hit with a winning combination, your win will be paid at 144 times the stated amount! A very nice hit indeed. Naturally, when you line up all three of these special symbols, you win the top jackpot.

THE MUNSTERS™

In keeping with the currently popular trend to take existing television icons and other generally familiar characters, this new IGT game uses the old TV family the Munsters as the main theme. All the popular characters from the TV show are there: Herman, Lily, Marilyn, and Grandpa. The game also features creepy credits with "fluttering Bat reel symbols."

The two main features of this game are the availability of the Herman Wild symbol, which substitutes for other symbols, and the Munsters 5X Pay symbol. Whenever the Herman head appears, this symbol will substitute for the others. When the Munsters 5X Pay symbol shows up on a payline with a winning combination, that pay is multiplied five times, and when two of these symbols are hit with any other symbol which makes a winning combination, that pay is then multiplied twenty-five times. As is common with these kinds of games, the top jackpot is paid when all three of the Munsters 5X Pay symbols are hit on the active payline.

SLINGO™

What will they think of next? This is a brand-new game, and one which you will be seeing a lot in your favorite casino. It's a three-reel slot machine, with the added feature of an LCD screen on which bonus games are awarded and played. The game is based on the very popular *Ten Times Pay*™ and *Double Diamond*™ games and features a bonus game which is a combination of slots and bingo—hence the term *Slingo*™. Here's how it works.

When a *Slingo*™ symbol lands on the third reel, with maximum coins bet, a bonus slot *Slingo*™ game begins. The LCD screen mounted on the top right of the machine's display, above the reels, presents a five-column, five-row bingo-like card with video reel numbers beneath each column. You start the game with ten spins and twelve of the twenty-five spaces covered. The object of the game, then, is to cover the remaining numbers on the card. If a number in a particular column matches the corresponding number on the video reel, the game automatically covers it and awards you bonus credits. When five numbers are covered vertically, horizontally, or diagonally (just like in a bingo game) you will hit the *Slingo*™ bonus and more credits will add up to your wins.

The entire game is packed with ways to earn credits. For

The great new *Slingo*™ reel slot machine.

example, if the Cherub lands on the video reel, the game then covers a number in that column and you will receive double credits for that spin. Hitting a Joker means the game covers numbers top to bottom or completes a *Slingo*™. If three or more Jokers land during one spin, the jackpot winnings increase. Then, if you hit a Bonus Spin symbol, you earn an additional free spin. In addition, the Gold Coin symbol counts for two extra credits. The Devil symbol, however, will take away an extra spin unless the Cherub also lands on the line during that same spin. Finally, if you cover all of the numbers on the *Slingo*™ card, you will get 50 credits and then 50 additional credits for each remaining spin.

Progressives

A "progressive" is a slot machine which is part of a linked chain of slot machines, all of which contribute to the same jackpot. These machines may be in several different casinos, and even in different cities throughout the same state. In some gaming jurisdictions, these progressives may even be linked among casinos in several different states. You can easily identify a progressive by looking at the digital display meter, which shows the top jackpot amount. If this meter is open-ended, meaning that the amount of the top jackpot continues to grow as the machines are played, then this is a progressive. Now all you have to do is figure out whether this is a statewide progressive, often called a multi-link progressive, or an in-house progressive.

Statewide, or multi-link, progressives can be found not only in different casinos, but also in casinos in different cities, or even states. The in-house progressives are similar, but are only linked to other machines in the same casino, or in casinos owned and/or operated by the same company. In this chapter, I will limit discussion to the multi-link progressives.

By far the most popular of all progressive machines made by IGT are the *Megabucks*® and *Quartermania* ™ machines. IGT pioneered this system and broke ground not only in casino and player acceptance of these games, but also in legislative and regulatory matters. Without their efforts and innovative thinking, we might never have had the *Megabucks*® millionaires, nor the hundreds of *Quartermania*® winners.

Big slot wins are usually publicized in the local media, and quite often also in the national media. The world's biggest slot machine jackpots have been hit on *Megabucks*® machines—more than $34 million in one case, and many others from the "mere" $3 million, $5 million, $10 million, and up. Needless to say, hits like this are quite life-altering. Similarly so for *Quartermania*®. Many winners have walked away with hundreds of thousands of dollars for the mere investment of 50¢ per spin.

Like the *Quartermania*® machines, the *Megabucks*® used to be four-reel machines, based on the reel slot machine concept I described earlier. Lately, most of the *Megabucks*® machines have gone to three reels, while many of the *Quartermania*® machines have remained as four-reelers, although there are plenty of three-reel machines to be found in most casinos. There is little difference in your ability to win the top jackpot on either of these games. Yes, the four-reel machines are somewhat harder to hit, but you should remember that the odds of winning are already part of the program on which these games operate. Therefore, your chances of hitting the top jackpot are just about the same on either the four- or the three-reel machines. The jackpot event itself is entirely random, and no one knows at any time when, or where, it will hit. Simply put, you have to be very, very lucky to hit the jackpot at just the right time.

These games also feature a variety of smaller payoffs, and even secondary progressive jackpots. There are also jackpot pays on the base game itself. Many of these machines are a version of the *Red, White & Blue* ™ machines we discussed earlier. Others are versions of the popular *Double Diamond*™ or *Triple Diamond*™ series. There are also the *Five Times Pay* ™ and the *Ten Times Pay*™ machines as the base game linked to these progressives. The look of the machine, or its base game, really doesn't matter. What does matter is whether the machine says *"Megabucks"*® on it, or *"Quartermania"*®, and has the distinct IGT logo. If the machine you are looking at has these symbols, then this is the true *Megabucks*® or *Quartermania*® machine, and you are about to play the best and most popular progressives in the world. Because these games are already widely known, I will not show them in photographs. Instead I want to show you some of the newest multi-link progressives.

WHEEL OF FORTUNE®

This game is one of the most popular casino slot machines ever produced. Unless you have been locked away on some remote island, or a mountain, for the past twenty years, you have seen the television show called *Wheel of Fortune*®. Based on this hugely successful show, IGT has produced a slot machine game which is a hybrid. This means it is a combination of a basic three-reel slot machine, with the addition of an extra component mounted to this machine, and linked together with it, to provide for an additional winning opportunity. In this case, that extra event is a roulette-style wheel, similar to the wheel in the TV show game. This is activated when you land the "spin" symbol on the third reel, with maximum coin play. Once this happens, chimes will sound and the machine prompts you to press a large circular lit button marked "spin." When you press this, the wheel above your head will start to spin. Eventually, as in the TV game show, the wheel will come to a stop and the protruding spoke, known as a rabbit's foot, will mark the amount you have won.

This great game was also popular as a stand-alone game, but the progressive feature made the game a national hit. Just about everyone who has ever been to a casino will have seen one, and probably played one. The game is offered as a quarter version, taking three coins, and as a $1 and a $5 version, each taking two coins as maximum bet.

There are a variety of jackpots which you can hit. Of course, the top jackpot is the progressive, awarded to you when you line up all three of the *Wheel of Fortune®* symbols on the payline, maximum coin bet.

The great *Wheel of Fortune®* progressive slot machine.

These machines come in a variety of the most popular IGT reel slots, and are prominent in any casino.

SINATRA™

Well, I guess it had to happen. Ol' Blue Eyes himself, Mr. Music, the *man*. Francis Albert Sinatra, known to the whole

world simply as Frank, and known on this new slot machine just as *Sinatra*™. Sinatra was not only a great singer and a movie star, but also a famed Las Vegas entertainer. His showbiz pals, Dean Martin, Sammy Davis Jr., Peter Lawford, and Joey Bishop, formed the famous Rat Pack, which frolicked and played to sold-out audiences in the Sands showroom in the early 1960s. Those were the days!

Sinatra has been immortalized in song, in music, in folklore—and now in slot machines. These games are designed around various themes from Sinatra's life and performances. There is a slot machine titled "Los Angeles" which shows Frank in his Hollywood days and one called "Chicago" which shows him in his club days. Of course, this

The new *Sinatra*™*Chicago* progressive reel slot machine.

wouldn't be a series if it didn't include "New York", and there is indeed a machine showing Frank against the backdrop of the Big Apple. Finally there is a machine called "Las

Vegas", which shows Frank in his prime as the entertainer of Las Vegas. No other singer has so epitomized what Las Vegas can be except perhaps, Elvis and Wayne Newton.

This game is a progressive, with a minimum starting jackpot amount of $200,000. Each machine also has a great stereophonic sound system which does justice to the medley of Sinatra songs which the machines play. This gives the game a center stage of its own, as well as providing terrific entertainment.

Each of the four stylized games features one of the four most popular IGT slot machines. These are all three-reel, single-payline machines, making them among the best and most easily played and understood reel slot machine games available. In each of the four "cities," the *Sinatra*™ symbol matches any other symbol and acts as a multiplier. Any three-symbol combination of the *Sinatra*™ or the base-theme multipliers will land that theme's major award for the number of coins wagered. With a one-coin bet, you can win the top jackpot when you line up three of the *Sinatra*™ symbols, but to win the *MegaJackpot*™ progressive, you must wager the maximum coins. If you achieve that same hit, you will win the progressive annuity. This is the minimum $200,000 jackpot which, of course, grows and grows until it is hit. Because it is an annuity, it will be paid in annual installments upon the verification of your win. This is its only drawback, but if you get the hit, well, why complain about the nice paycheck you will now receive every year?

REGIS' CASH CLUB™

"Mr. Showbiz" has his own slot machine, and what a game it is. Not only is this game a progressive, but it combines a multi-line reel slot machine with a video slot machine and four video bonus screens. Plus, of course, the progressive jackpot which starts at a respectably "cool" $1 million. The machine itself is tall and very distinctive and you can't miss it. Here's how it works.

The game integrates state-of-the-art video animation on an LCD screen, mounted over the main reel slot game window, with sophis-ticated mechanical engi-neering wizardry. There are numerous bonuses and other means of winning. One of the primary objectives is to move up the *Column of Cash* to obtain that bonus. The higher you get, the more money you win. Any three *Column of Cash* symbols on any payline on the base game will initiate this bonus. You will be presented with five button choices and four "picks." Each button will allow you to move up the *Column of Cash* for an undisclosed amount of spaces, or it gives you an-other special option.

The "Up 1 Level," "Up 2 Levels," and "Up 3 Levels" buttons will move you up the *Column of Cash* accord-ingly. The "Free Pick" but-ton will give you another pick. The "Top 2" button will reveal two of the lower-values selections, and you must then choose between

The terrific *Regis' Cash Club*™ pro-gressive reel slot machine.

the two remaining higher-value selections. Finally, the "Trade Up" button prompts you to select another button. If your second selection is an "Up 3 Levels" button, you then move up accordingly. If your second selection is either the "Up 1 Level" or the "Up 2 Levels" option, you can either keep what you got or try again.

If you get the "Big Check" bonus, which you will hit whenever any two or more of the Big Check symbols appear on any payline, you will see Regis himself. He will write you a bonus check for your credits right then and there. Sometimes, however, Regis decides that the bonus check isn't big enough, so he will simply replace it with a bigger amount. But that's not all.

When you line up all five of Regis's symbols on the ninth payline, with maximum coins bet, you will win that big progressive. This, of course, means you have joined *Regis' Cash Club*™ and are now the newest slot millionaire from IGT.

The *Regis' Cash Club*™ video LCD Free Pick screen.

THE PRICE IS RIGHT™

This is a video slot machine, but because this game is also a progressive I am including it here. This will also be the case for the *I Love Lucy*® video progressive, which I will discuss in this chapter.

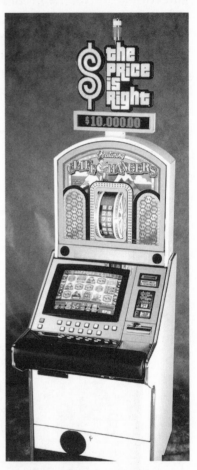

The *Price Is Right*™ machines are based on the IGT *MegaJackpots*™ system. There are two versions of this game, one with the Cliff Hanger Bonus and the other with the Plinko Bonus. Both games also feature the Showcase Showdown Bonus as well.

The base game is the nine-line video slot machine based on the *The Price Is Right*™ theme. The next two versions of the game in the development of this theme feature the addition of these bonuses plus the progressive jackpot, which starts at $10,000.

When you reach the Showcase Showdown Bonus, you will receive up to two spins from the top-box reel.

The new *The Price Is Right*™ progressive reel slot machine.

If the spin results in 55 to 100 credits, the game's stage is now set for some big bonus fun in the main Showcase round. In this main round, you get to pick on-screen price tags, each of which reveals a prize amount paid in the total number of credits shown on the tag. Some tags add extra bonus credits to your prize package, and one tag is a multiplier which can multiply your win up to five times. When you reveal the values of all the prize tags in that package, you will be awarded the package's total bonus credits. If the total spin amount was not over 100 credits, you will win the total spin amount multiplied by the line bet amount. Otherwise, you will still receive a consolation spin. If your spin results in exactly 100 credits, you get an extra spin that could mean even more credits for you.

The Cliff Hanger Bonus and the Plinko Bonus are the two main features which separate the two games. You can tell which game you are playing by looking at the top of the game itself, where it will say either "Plinko" or "Cliff-hanger." Otherwise, all the other features of the games are the same as described here.

In the Cliff Hanger Bonus, the object is for you to help your yodeling climber climb up the side of the mountain. You do this by picking up to three price tags. Each tag reveals the number of steps the climber will take. The farther the climber goes, the more credits you get. But if the climber

The Price Is Right™ Plinko bonus screen.

goes over the edge and falls down the cliff, you will have to settle for the consolation credits (which aren't shabby at all). Even if your climber goes over the edge, you will always win something in this bonus round.

In the Plinko Bonus round, you will first receive one Plinko chip. You then try to get as many as three more chips by selecting three products from groups of two on the bonus screen. The more chips you find, the more chances you have to get the biggest Plinko bonus. After you have collected all the chips you can get, you indicate where to drop them by touching your finger over that specific area at the top of the Plinko board. You do this one by one for all the chips you were able to collect during the earlier part of this bonus round. The Plinko chip then ambles its way down the Plinko board, bouncing around as it hits the spokes. Eventually it will land in a pocket which designates the bonus amount you will win. And so on for all the chips which you were able to collect for this bonus round.

The traditional Plinko game used to be a popular carnival game. The game was simply a board with nails protruding from it, and with pockets below. A rubber ring, or a ball, was dropped in from the top, gravity took over, and eventually the ring, or ball, bounced its way down to the bottom and came to rest in a pocket, which then designated your win. This version of *The Price Is Right*™, with the Plinko Bonus, is very similar to that game in the Plinko Bonus round. I like that version of this progressive better than the others, but that's just my own personal preference. All the games in this series are great fun and offer terrific wins.

I LOVE LUCY®

In keeping with the other great IGT games based on popular themes and television shows, this is a five-reel twelve-line video slot machine which is also a bonus game as well as a progressive. All the popular characters from the TV show are represented in this game, but the most fun you will have is when you land on the Chocolate Factory Bonus.

If you remember the TV episode on which this bonus is based, you already know what I mean. In the event that you missed this episode, I will attempt to describe it briefly. In this scene, Lucy and Ethel are workers in a chocolate factory. Their job is to wrap chocolate treats which are coming down a conveyor belt. At first, all is well, but the conveyor belt soon starts to run faster. And then faster. The faster the belt runs, the more difficult it is for Lucy and Ethel to wrap the chocolates. They try to eat as many as they can while trying to wrap as many of the others as possible. In this bonus round, the faster the conveyor belt runs and the more chocolates the ladies eat, the more bonus credits you will win. You've got to see it to believe it!

There is another bonus called the Classic Moments Bonus. When three of these

This is the video *I Love Lucy*® progressive reel slot machine.

The *I Love Lucy*® Chocolate Factory bonus screen.

symbols land on any active payline, the game takes you to the bonus screen where you have a choice of three classic scenes from the TV show. Pick one, it then plays in glorious black and white, and your bonus credits are awarded to your credit meter.

And yes, of course, this is a progressive. The jackpot is achieved when you land all of the heart-shaped *I Love Lucy*® symbols on the winning active payline. The top jackpot starts at $200,000 and is paid instantly (based on the regulatory requirements of the gaming jurisdiction in which you happened to have hit the jackpot).

I also wish to let you know that this game is available as a 2-coin, three-reel slot machine. You can't miss it because it will have the red heart-shaped *I Love Lucy*® sign on the glass at the top of the machine. Both games are progressives, and both are sure to be very entertaining. I happen to prefer the video game, but, again, that's my own personal preference. Many times, the 2-coin game may be as great an option as the video one.

QUARTERMANIA®

Yes, I already mentioned the *Megabucks*® and *Quartermania*® slots, but I'd like to briefly mention two new versions of the *Quartermania*® game.

As I will discuss in the next chapter, IGT has a terrific new video game called *Texas Tea*™. I've played this game many times, and I'll tell you about it later. Right now I want to let you know that IGT has made a *Quartermania*® reel slot machine progressive game based on this *Texas Tea*™ video game. This reel game, called *Triple Texas Tea*™, is a three-reel five-line game and is based on the progressive *MegaJackpots*™ system pioneered by IGT.

This version of the game features the famed "Texas dialogue," a series of cute sayings spoken by the main game character, Texas Ted. When three Big Oil Bonus symbols line up on any played line, the bonus shifts to the mechanical top box where three special reels protrude from the machine. Texas Ted and his armadillo from Amarillo appear in the Video Fluorescent Display (VFD) and offer you a great Texas greeting. They then walk you through the bonus round. Don't forget that when two of the Big Oil Bonus symbols are hit along with one of the *Triple Texas Tea*™ symbols, the whole bonus is tripled!

Not to be outdone by Texas Ted, a devilish new character explodes on the scene in the newest version of this *Quartermania*® progressive, called *Diablo Diamond*™. This game is based on the popular *Double Diamond*™ theme, but with a new twist which includes a three-reel five-line game with protruding bonus reels, great sound effects, the familiar "diamond" bonus award structure, and that impish little Diablo character who acts as the initiator of the bonus rounds.

When three Diablo characters line up on any played line, the bonus shifts to those protruding reels above the main game, similar to that in the *Triple Texas Tea*™ game. Here you will be greeted by the Diablo character and prompted to press the "spin" button to start the bonus round. The bonus game reels contain bonus values and diamonds and spin at random, one at a time. When a reel stops on a value, that

value is added to the credits-won amount. When a reel stops on a diamond, five credits are awarded and that reel becomes inactive. The remaining reels continue to spin and land on bonus values, until all three reels eventually are stopped by the appearance of that diamond, at which point the bonus game ends and all wins are accumulated.

HARLEY-DAVIDSON®

You will be rumbling your way to great wins on this progressive video machine from IGT, based on a true American legend. This is a twelve-line game, with the added features of bonus screen awards, as well as the spinning motorcycle wheel mounted above the main game. Here's how it works.

You get the Eagle bonus when three, four, or five of the Eagle symbols land any-

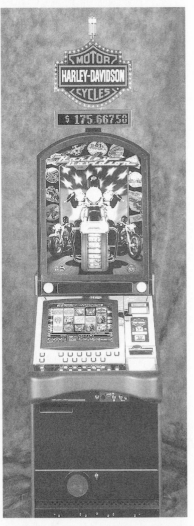

The rumbling new *Harley-Davidson®* progressive reel slot machine.

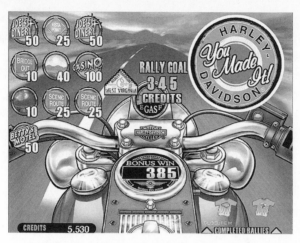

The *Harley-Davidson®* Road Rally winner's screen.

where on the reels. Pick an Eagle, and it will reveal your bonus and you will win that amount. Getting to the Road Rally requires you to hit three or more of these symbols consecutively on any active played payline. Now you can get ready for the born-to-ride easy-rider rally and accumulate your bonus credits. There are three rallies to complete. If you make the rally goals on all three destinations without running out of spins, you automatically qualify for the Great American Rally bonus. Once in this bonus round, you get to select your favorite Rally T-shirt icon which reveals even more credits you have won, or it will reveal a multiplier which will multiply your wins up to four times. During these bonus games, the number of spins you have left is shown on your gas gauge. You should also keep an eye out for the spinning motorcycle wheel above the main screen, because when that starts rolling you will win even more.

THE $1,000,000 PYRAMID™

I've saved the best for last. This one is again based on a popular television game show of the same name. Although it is not technically a progressive, because it pays a fixed amount, nonetheless the amount is an instant win of $1 million, and that I think should qualify this game for inclusion among the big-money progressives. But please note that this game does *not* progress past the $1 million top jackpot, which is a fixed amount.

This is a five-reel nine-line game with a maximum bet option of 90 coins per spin. Along with many recognizable and popular prizes from the game show, this video slot machine features a chance for you to become an instant millionaire. The jackpot is paid instantly, upon verification of the win.

When you hit the "double" symbol, which features the face of the TV show's host, your wins are doubled. If you hit five of the diamond symbols, then you win the top jackpot for the reel game. When you hit three Winner's Circle Bonus symbols on reels one, two, and three, correctly lined up in sequence on an active played payline, you will be transported to the Pyramid bonus round where you will get the chance to win the $1 million prize. This prize can be won only with maximum coins bet; however, you will still be able to get bonus pays regardless of how many total coins you played, as long as you hit the correct sequence which launched you into this bonus round.

Once you enter the bonus round, the game show's host will guide you through the rest of the game. Simply put, you will see a pyramid with a lot of blue blocks. You will be asked to pick seven of these blocks. This you do by touching each one, one at a time, by placing your finger on the screen over the blue block which you wish to select. When you select a block, it will turn over and reveal either a bonus amount by displaying a figure with the number of credits you have won, or an icon which symbolizes the golden pyramid. This continues for as long as you have selections to make. When you have made the final, seventh, selection, the bonus round is over and your wins will be awarded.

Depending on how many pyramids you have uncovered along with any numerically shown credit amounts won, the game will award you a multiple win. To win the top $1 million jackpot, three things must happen: You must wager the maximum coins; you must hit the required Winner's Circle Bonus symbols to gain access to the Pyramid bonus round; and you will have to pick all seven golden pyramids. If you do, then you are an instant millionaire.

One thing I really like about this machine is that after you have selected all your bonus round pyramid blocks, the game will actually turn over all the remaining golden pyramids so that you can see where they all were. This will let you see how close you came to being an instant millionaire!

Video Slots

Video slot machines are the wave of the future. Actually, they are already the wave of the present, due to the fast-expanding computer technology. With each passing month, new and better computer chips become available. More memory, faster processors, bigger capacity, more available options. The makers of video games are on the cutting edge of entertainment.

IGT video game engineers are the pioneers in video slot machine games and technology. Because of their foresight and the head start this gave them, most of the video slot machines now in casinos are from IGT. In this chapter, I showcase some of these great games. It isn't possible to show them all, but the ones I have selected for this chapter show just how far video gaming has been able to expand. These games offer some of the best payback percentages of all the slot machines you will play on your casino trip, as well as being hugely entertaining, and great fun to play. They offer a tremendous variety of play and pay options, as well as numerous bonus games.

If you have never played a video slot machine before, I would certainly encourage you to find one in your favorite casino on your next trip, or look for any slot machine which displays the IGT logo and be assured that you are about to play one of the best games you can find.

The games I have selected for this chapter are in no particular order. Because there are so many of them, I will limit my descriptions to the game itself and how it plays, and show photographs wherever possible. One of the advantages of these video slots is the fact that they all contain "help" screens which explain the game, as well as a "pay" screen which shows the pays and how you win and on which symbols. This is also true for the bonus games. If you see something you don't know and would like to find out more details, you can look it up on the machine's help screen as well.

Let's begin with one of the creepiest, most frightening machines yet to be unleashed upon the unsuspecting slot players in casinos everywhere.

THE ADDAMS FAMILY™

No self-respecting chapter on video machines would be worthy of the effort if we didn't frighten you a little. This video slot machine is based on the cartoon characters created by Charles Addams. You can experience spooky delights as this game brings you ever closer to a more frightening experience. Perhaps we should say "rewarding" experience as well, because there are many ways to win on this game.

It is a five-reel nine-line game with a maximum bet of 45 coins. Like all IGT video machines, it features stunning graphics and top-notch sound, as well as a monitor with superior video resolution; you will be able to see the game clearly and enjoy it without having to squint.

The bonus features are combined into three separate themes. First, the Market Madness bonus round consists of the Market Madness and Train bonuses. When three or more of the Market Madness symbols hit on any active payline, Gomez and Thing will guide you through an offer-based game with multiple chances to win big awards. To get the Train Bonus, two Train symbols must first land on the top, middle, or bottom of both the first and fifth reels. When this happens, you are into the bonus round. In the Train Bonus, two trains appear to be heading for a collision. Thing, however, saves the day and awards you winning bonus credits.

In the second bonus feature, the Pick to Win theme includes the Train Bonus. In the Pick to Win feature, you must first land three, four, or five of these bonus symbols on any payline. When these cause a scatter pay, they launch Lurch's Pick to Win bonus. Lurch then asks you to pick from a series of dollar signs ($$) to accumulate credits throughout multiple rounds of bonus play. Of course, the Train Bonus feature works the same as previously described, and is also available in the Pick to Win game.

The third of the three bonus games is the Fry Fester theme, which features the Fry Fester and the Rock, Paper, Scissors bonuses. Any three Fry Fester symbols in any position start this great bonus. As the bonus continues, you will get the chance to re-energize Fester. He's feeling a little low on energy, and you will give him a boost by selecting bonuses. The electricity mounts as the bonus values increase. The other part of this bonus feature is the Rock, Paper, Scissors game. If any wild Thing™ symbol lands on any active payline along with any of the correctly lined-up Thing symbols, you will then get the chance to play Thing at a game of Rock, Paper, Scissors. The more you win, the higher the multiplied wins—anywhere from two times to ten times the win. It's a fun game to play and will keep you amused for a long time, as well as providing you with some serious winning opportunities.

DIAMOND CINEMA™ FEATURING MARILYN MONROE ™

I'm not ashamed to say it: I was in love with Marilyn Monroe. I was eight years old when she died, and I only began to appreciate who she was much later in life, when I grew up and started to watch those great old films. Now IGT has made a series of video slots based around the theme of the old silver screen days. This series of machines is called the *Diamond Cinema™*, and the two games I will showcase here are this one, *Marilyn Monroe™*, and one based on the famed duo of actors in the classic film *Casablanca*, Humphrey Bogart and Ingrid Bergman.

The Marilyn Monroe game features various bonuses and many ways to win. When a wild symbol lands on the second and fourth reels, the whole reel becomes animated. This shows the legendary scene where Marilyn's flowing

The stylish new *Diamond Cinema™ featuring Marilyn Monroe™* video slot machine.

white dress blows up around her waist as the subway train passes below and causes air to blow up through the grating. This is the classic scene from the film *The Seven Year Itch*, which Marilyn Monroe made while married to baseball's legendary hitter Joe DiMaggio, who absolutely hated this scene.

This was the only scene in the movie that was shot on a Hollywood soundstage. The rest of the film was made on location in New York. But when they were trying to film this scene on a public street, there were so many people watching them make that scene, and so many of them kept yelling at Marilyn and whistling "whoopee," that the director could not get the shot. Also, Marilyn's husband, Joe DiMaggio, kept yelling that he didn't want his wife to be shown "half naked" to the whole world. The actual scenes shot in New York on that street show Marilyn bare all the way to her waist and there is indeed a whole lot of Marilyn to be seen. In the end, these scenes were cut out of the film, and a very private scene was staged on a soundstage at the studio in Hollywood, which produced the very mild and timid scene we now see in the movie. Nevertheless, that scene is still considered racy, and as a sort of trademark of Marilyn's allure. Well, so much for reminiscing. Back to the game.

When three, four, or five of the Marilyn Bonus Magazine symbols land left to right on any active payline, you will get to play the Magazine Bonus. The voice of an actress impersonating Marilyn will then guide you through the bonus game. In this game, Marilyn's image is shown on the covers of twelve magazines. Touch the magazine cover, and each will reveal a credit value bonus, a credit value plus another pick, or a gift box. All the credit values accumulate as the round progresses. For each extra pick you reveal, Marilyn's voice will ask you to make another pick. And so on. If you get the gift box, you are then guided to the Gift Box Bonus. You will see a screen with several gift boxes. Pick a box and it will reveal your additional win credit value, which is then added to everything else you have won so far.

DIAMOND CINEMA™ FEATURING BOGART AND BERGMAN™

Rick's Café Americain, the intrigue, the love, the immortal song "As Time Goes By." Here's looking at you, kid. Once again IGT brings back the nostalgia of the silver screen, in this installment in the *Diamond Cinema*™ series of video slots.

This game has two main bonuses. When three piano symbols land on the middle reels of any row, they become animated and play the famous song "As Time Goes By." This is the As Time Goes By Bonus. When the song ends, you will win the amount of the credits shown on the screen. The Palace of Riches Bonus is triggered when three, four, or five *Bogart and Bergman*™ symbols land left to right on any active payline. You are then whisked away into a classic old movie theater where the

The new *Diamond Cinema*™ featuring *Bogart and Bergman*™ video slot machine.

impersonated voices of the *Bogart and Bergman*™ characters take you through the rest of the bonus round. During this round, starting with the bottom row, you will get to select a square from the on-screen grid. The squares reveal credit values, arrows, or *Bogart and Bergman*™ symbols. The credit values accumulate as the round progresses. If you reveal an arrow, you are then asked to select from the next row. If you find a *Bogart and Bergman*™ symbol, the game will now award you all of the credits on that row and you will be asked to keep selecting squares from the next row.

Once you reach the top row, you will be asked to select only one square. This can reveal either a credit value or glittering green jewels. If you uncover the credit value, then this amount of your win is added to all your other wins so far. If you uncover the green jewels, you will then be transported to the Gem Bonus. The voices of the characters will ask you to pick from nine gemstones to reveal your additional credits.

I DREAM OF JEANNIE™

This delightful television show has always been one of my favorites. Like any teenager in the mid-1960s, I had an awful crush on Barbara Eden, the actress who played Jeannie in the TV show. I still watch all the episodes I can find on TV and still find enjoyment in that classic comedy. They just don't make them like this anymore.

This game comes packaged in hot pink, of course, with the cartoon illustration of Jeannie on the front of the machine's cabinet. The game is a five-reel nine-line video slot machine, which in this version features the Jeannie Bottle Bonus. You may have already played a similar game where there is a bonus wheel mounted at the top of the game, similar to the *Wheel of Fortune*® game. In that game, you get to spin the wheel when you hit the required combination on any active payline. This game doesn't have the big wheel at the top, but instead has a big Jeannie bottle mounted over the machine, although there is a version of this game which *does* have a bonus spin wheel.

There are actually two bonuses in this game. The Make a Wish Bonus starts when three, four, or five of these "wish" symbols land on adjacent reels left to right. The voice of Jeannie congratulates you and asks you to select one or more bottles. If you achieved entry into this bonus round by landing three of the "wish" symbols, then you will get to pick one bottle. You will get to pick two bottles if you landed four of the "wish" symbols, and you will get to pick three bottles if you landed all five of the "wish" symbols to get into this round. Each time you touch the bottle during this round, it turns into a puff of pink Jeannie dust; this reveals the amount of credits you have won.

The Jeannie Bottle Bonus starts when you land three, four, or five of the "bottle" symbols on adjacent reels. The screen shows a lot of Jeannie bottles on a beach. Each bottle reveals a bonus credit win. Keep touching the bottles for as long as you can, but when you touch a bottle which reveals the words "Sorry, Master" spoken by Jeannie, the round is over. All the credits you have won so far are now added to your other wins.

TEXAS TEA™

I have played this new game many times and it is not only great fun, but it also pays very well. I mentioned this game briefly in the section on progressives, when we discussed the new IGT *Quartermania*® machine based around this *Texas Tea*™ popular video machine concept.

This game is a five-reel nine-line video slot machine with some of the craziest characters you will ever find in a

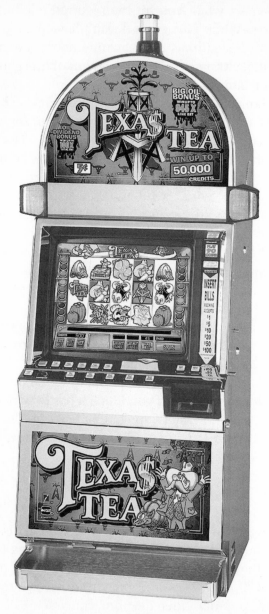

The great new *Texas Tea*™ video slot machine.

video slot machine. You will never tire of playing it, not only because of the homely Texas drawl of the Texas Ted main character, but also because of the armadillo from Amarillo, mooing cows and—well, all the rest. It's so funny!

Three or more of the Texas Ted symbols trigger the Oil Dividend bonus. When you hit this, the screen changes to the view of Ted's office where he is about to write you an oil dividend check. This check sails from his desk and reveals the amount of your credit bonus. And it's always as big as Texas! The Big Oil bonus starts when three or more of the oil derricks land on any active payline. Once this happens, the screen rumbles and shakes, and the "black gold" oil starts to ooze from all around the screen until it covers the entire screen. When it washes away you are transported to another bonus screen where you will see a map of Texas divided into eight sections. Each section has a counter. At the bottom right of the screen are two additional counters. One keeps a score of how many credits you won during this round, and the other keeps a score of how much you won overall.

The *Texas Tea*™ winner's screen, as Ted takes his hat off to you after your win.

Texas Ted will now ask you to pick a region and place an oil rig on it. Once you have placed all the derricks you can on the selected regions, they each start pumping oil. As they pump, your profits are accumulated on the counter in each region. This goes on for quite a while, as each derrick starts and stops, while another one starts and stops, and so on, until all wells run dry. By that time you will have accumulated a lot of credits, which are displayed on each region's credit meter, as well as added to the overall credit meter below.

With frequent hits, and very frequent bonus hits, and very nice payoffs, this is one of the best video games you can find.

MY RICH UNCLE™

In keeping with the "let's get rich" theme, here is a great game in which you can become one of the people who "inherit" a fortune from your rich uncle. This is a five-reel nine-line video slot machine in which you are trying to get your share of the inheritance when Uncle Mega Bux passes on and leaves a fortune to be divided among his greedy relatives.

When three, four, or five of the "Will" symbols land on any active payline, you are transported into the attorney's office where the will is being read. First, however, you get to pick the lucky inheritor. You touch one of the hopeful relatives, and then select from several items which the character you selected really wants. Then you wait to see what they have inherited as the attorney reads who gets what. As each of the items is awarded to the relatives, for each one which is received by your character, you win a corresponding credit amount. If your character gets the item you have selected as their favorite, then your accumulated bonus is doubled.

There is also another bonus to be had. Whenever you hit three, four, or five "Safe" symbols as a scatter pay, you will be prompted to select one of these safes. It will then unlock and reveal your bonus amount. Of course there are plenty of sound effects, and the characters jab at each other with barbs about their greed. It all adds to the overall fun experience of playing.

ELVIRA®—MISTRESS OF THE DARK™

Based on the popular late-night television horror-show actress of the same name, this new video slot machine features an entire variety of creepy creatures and pays. This is a distinctive slot machine: it is very tall and has a statue of *Elvira®* sitting seductively at the top of the machine. Below that statue is a spiderweb-style wheel, similar to the *Wheel of Fortune®* wheel, where various bonus amounts are shown. Below that is the actual game screen itself, and the entire machine is further adorned with photos of a reclining *Elvira®* beckoning you to step into her web.

The Midnight Matinee Bonus starts when two of the symbols land on the first and fifth reels. *Elvira®* then appears between them and explains the rules of the game. She will ask you to pick one of the five movie titles shown on the TV screen. The top TV displays the feature film *Elvira's Haunted Hills*, and a premultiplied credit value. The remaining TVs show a variety of "B" movie titles. A menu of four premultiplied credit values indicates what you might win depending on the choices you make among the bottom four movies. After you make your selection, the TV becomes bigger on the screen and plays a movie. There are fifteen different movies, so chances are you will not know which one you get, even if you have played the game a lot. After the movie clip stops, the Rating Skulls bonus round starts where you will get the chance to double your bonus with no risk.

The Web of Winnings Bonus is another feature of this hugely entertaining game. When you land three Spinning Spider symbols on any active payline, *Elvira®* will ask you to pick a symbol which will determine whether you will get three, four, or five spins on the Web of Winnings wheel bonus game. Once you have selected the icon and found out how many spins you have won, *Elvira®* settles into her chair and asks you to press the "spin" button, which starts the top wheel spinning. The bonus wheel will award you the number of credits displayed on the winning selection. However, when you land on Elvira's Chest, you get the chance to pick one of three bonus chests. Whichever chest you pick, the top opens and a creature pops up to show you the bonus win.

Finally, there's the Deadhead Scatter and Shatter Bonus. When three "deadhead" symbols land anywhere on reels one, three, and five, these disembodied heads animate and bob inside their glass jars in time with the song lyric "I ain't got nobody." At this

The new *Elvira®* video slot machine.

This is the *Elvira*® Midnight Matinee bonus introduction screen.

point your job is to select one of these deadheads by touching it with your finger. Once you have picked your deadhead, the head shatters the glass jar and reveals your winning amount of credits.

This very ingenious game offers more varieties of wins than you can imagine and will keep you entertained for a long time.

RICHARD PETTY DRIVING EXPERIENCE™

Buckle up, start the engine, grab the wheel. We're off to a NASCAR adventure with top driver Richard Petty. This is truly a high-octane game, with five reels and nine lines. It is an interactive game with digital stereo sound and video footage of professional stock car racing with the *Richard Petty Driving Experience*™ on the high banks of a super speedway.

Race-inspired reel icons include colored and checkered flags, animated helmets, gas cans, tachometers, and tires, plus a wild trophy symbol that substitutes for symbols, except the scatter and bonus symbols. To get to the bonus race round, you must first line up three or more of the race car symbols on an active payline. Then, at the drop of the flag, you get to take charge of Richard Petty's red, white, and blue number 43 race car, maneuvering around the racetrack, passing up to eight other cars, and reaching the finish line where your bonus win credits will be revealed.

The new *Richard Petty Driving Experience*™ video slot machine.

EVEL KNIEVEL™

In keeping with the heart-pounding thrills of IGT's new series of video slot machines, this brand-new game features a host of Evel's best jumps and bonuses. This is a five-reel fifteen line game which will thrill you just as Evel Knievel's stunts did. If you are a slot thrill-seeker, then this is the game for you. State-of-the-art 3-D video animation and actual film footage of Evel's famous stunts will keep you spellbound. The game features a powerful symbol set, with stars and stripes adorning helmets and cycles, hearts, and Evel's number 1 symbol, in addition to animated attractions such as *Evel Knievel's*™ EK logo, the Sky Cycle, standing and sitting "wheelies," Evel's Wreck symbols, and even more. The base game even boasts Evel's own gravel-voiced quips about various hits and misses.

There are several bonuses in this terrific game. The Dare Devil Bonus starts when three of the Dare Devil scatter symbols appear anywhere on the first three reels. When you enter this bonus round, the first scene you will see is a panoramic sweep of a stadium, showing the ramps and obstacles Evel will use in his jump. When the stage is set, the camera angle shifts to show the view from Evel's helmet-cam as he sits astride his bike at the top of the tall tower, looking down the ramp. For the first Dare Devil bonus jump, a single "Jump!" button flashes on your screen. Evel then offers you verbal game instructions and prompts you to be courageous, and take risks for the rewards. On-screen messages ask you to push the button and provide you with game strategy plans as well as jump statistics. When you push the button the engine roars and a split screen shows you three different views of the animated jump from three front-row cameras. Evel then races down the ramp and takes the jump. If he crashes, the bonus round is over and you will be paid a nice consolation win. If he lands safely, you will then be asked to press the button marked "Bail!" if you want to collect your winnings right then and there. Or you can press the "Jump!" button again and try for bigger wins. If you opt for the "Bail!" button, you then get whatever credits you have won up to that moment and the game is over. You will also be able to see what you would have won if you had selected the second jump. Or, perhaps, you will get to see that you would have crashed on the second jump and not won anything more.

If you do take the chance and press the "Jump!" button for the second, third, or fourth round, this launches Evel on progressively more perilous, and potentially more rewarding, runs down the ramp. A consolation prize is offered for any bonus-ending wreck, and another chance to "Jump!" or

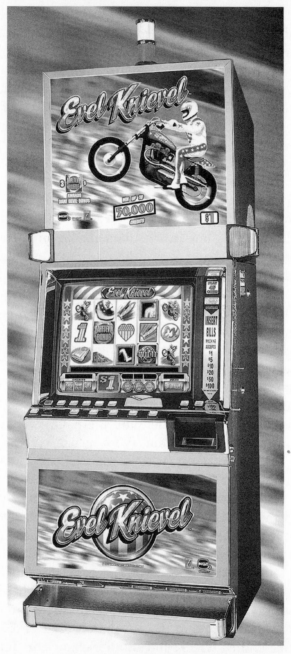

The new *Evel Knievel*™ video slot
machine.

The *Evel Knievel*™ Jump! bonus game screen.

"Bail!" is offered after each successful jump. You can make up to a total of four jumps.

The second bonus is called the X-Ray Bonus. To get to this bonus you must first hit three or more X-Ray symbols anywhere on the reels. Once you do, the screen turns a surgical green color, high-voltage sounds zap and sizzle, and the X-Ray icons animate, revealing Evel's broken body parts. You will get to pick one of these glowing X-Ray images, and it will reveal the amount of your bonus. But there is also a bonus within this bonus. When you are lucky enough to pick the part which reveals the Win All symbol, then you will be paid every credit amount hidden behind every body part which you have landed on the screen.

The third and final bonus on this game is the Reality Check Bonus. This begins when landing and take-off jump-ramp symbols align on reels two and four, on either side of a variety of jump obstacle symbols on the middle, third, reel. These can be cars, pickup trucks, tractors, buses, or whatever symbols are available on the game for this bonus. A screen then pops up showing actual film footage of one of four different *Evel Knievel*™ famous jumps. You might see

Evel soaring over the Snake River, through the air at the Cow Palace, flying across Wembley Stadium in London, or jumping over the famous fountains in Las Vegas. After the jump the bonus win credits are added to your win total, and Evel himself congratulates you for the jump and the win.

AUSTIN POWERS™

The spy-from-the-cold has come to the casino nearest you in the form of this exciting and superbly kitsch new video slot machine game. This is a five-reel nine-line game with all of the popular characters from the two movies that spawned this phenomenon. During the bonus rounds you will be flown back in time to an era where discos ruled and go-go boots were the height of fashion. Various clips from the two films will keep you amused as the famed Frau Farbissina keeps the game moving with her high-shrieking commands in her notoriously funny German accent. On top of this, the cast of the various bonus scenes changes each time you hit the bonus and so you will never tire of it because you will never know who, or what, you are about to get. Or get into.

The Fembot Bonus round starts when three Frau Farbissina bonus symbols land on reels 3, 4, and 5. Frau Farbissina yells, "Bring the Fembots," at which point the screen changes to that round and you are asked to pick a Fembot. When you choose either the left or the right Fembot, either will take her machine-gun halter to shoot out the amount of your bonus win on the screen. When you pick the middle Fembot, she will release a cloud of pink gas which reveals your win once it clears.

The Faces of Austin Bonus starts when four or more of the *Austin Powers*™ symbols land on any payline. Music plays and the symbols are highlighted on the screen. You are then prompted to select one of the symbols. When you

do, a film clip from one of
the two movies plays and
after it is finished, the screen
reveals your bonus win.

The Henchman Bonus
round begins when three Dr.
Evil symbols land on reels 1,
2, and 3. Dr. Evil sneers,
welcomes you to his lair,
and the Eliminate a Henchman bonus screen appears.
Here you will be asked to
"Replace Credits with Multiplier," which you do by selecting a Henchman, or more
Henchmen as you are al-
lowed by the prompts on the
game. Each time you select a
Henchman, he will fall back
into a flaming pit and reveal
that credit bonus. This value
is then crossed out and a
multiplier is revealed. Once

This is the groovy *Austin Powers™*
video slot machine.

you have selected and revealed all the multipliers, they are
added together. Then Frau Farbissina yells, "End of bonus,"
and the game reveals the remaining Henchmen's values.
These credit values are then added up, multiplied by the
final multiplier, and these wins added to your credit meter.

The Match Bonus round begins when you hit all five of
either the Felicity or the Vanessa Kensington symbols on
any active payline. This takes you to the Select and Match
bonus screen where the game prompts you to select symbols. When a symbol is selected, a character appears and
says a line from one of the two *Austin Powers™* movies.
When a match is made, this is highlighted on the Match

This is the *Austin Powers* Fembots bonus screen.

and Win scoreboard. If you happen to select the Fat Bastard symbol, Frau Farbissina notifies you that you now can select only one more match and then the bonus round will be over. In addition, if you happen to uncover the Mojo symbol during this round, all of your wins are doubled.

LITTLE GREEN MEN™

Let's follow up the zany *Austin Powers*™ game with the *Little Green Men*™ from Mars, or whatever south-of-the-stars aliens they may be. In this five-reel nine-line video slot machine game, you get the chance to play the spaceman and abduct an Earthling. This is one of the two bonuses on this game. In the other you can earn extra credits by blasting alien flying saucers from the sky.

CLEOPATRA™

And finally, what better way to end this chapter than with an Egyptologist's dream game. The amateur archeologist in all slot players will delight in uncovering great pays and bonuses. This game can be found in a five-reel nine-line version, and even in a twenty-line version. Of course, the more lines you have, the better your chances for a really nice "Nile" win, so I'd recommend that you look for the 20-line game as your first choice. I like the biggest wins possible, and that's one of the reasons I like this game.

The *Cleopatra*™ symbol is wild and doubles any win amount in which it participates. The other reel symbols are taken directly from the hieroglyphs of ancient Egypt, including a scarab, a hieroglyphic eye, a flail, a cartouche, and a variety of stylized poker symbols. Animated flaming Sphinx symbols indicate scatter pays, and the *Cleopatra*™ Bonus allows you to win up to fifteen free games during which all pays are tripled. This one will keep you spellbound and entertained for a long time, and quite likely shower you with large wins.

There are many slot machines which will entice your fancy once you arrive in the casino. Learning all you can about them will give you the ideal perspective on how to play them.

Yes, there is a big world out there, but you need not be overwhelmed by the many slot machines and video games you will find. Good luck, and my best wishes as you find and play your own favorites.

Part Three

HOW TO BE A WINNER

Keys to Winning

Every slot player knows what "that certain feeling" means. It's that itch, that tingle, that gnawing at the back of your mind or hand, that "absolutely" indicates that *this* slot machine is about to *pay!* We've all had that feeling. Walking into a casino we are suddenly and mysteriously drawn to a particular machine, or a particular kind of machine, hearing the ringing and seeing the jackpot even as we reach for the money to put in the slot.

Are such "mysterious" or "psychic" moments real, or is this just a coincidence—the kind of "blind luck" which strikes some of us while leaving most of us untouched? I confess that I've had such feelings myself. I've even acted on them. I've seen other people act on them. Did I win? No. Did they win? Sometimes. Was it because of "that certain feeling"? Realistically, no. Was it just a sudden strike of pure luck? Mostly yes.

So, my friends ask me, how do *you* win? Is it luck? Sure, I am lucky, sometimes. But mostly it is *knowledge, patience, bankroll, selection, discipline,* and *win goal*—the Keys to

Winning. Put all those together, and *apply* them correctly, and you *become* lucky. At least that's what people will say when they watch you hit the jackpot and wonder how you did it, or how you can do it that often.

Many people look down upon slot players. They say that slots are a waste of money and that you can only win if you're lucky. To them I say, yes, I'm lucky—at least that's how *you* can understand it. Those of us who play slots the *smart* way *know* that our luck is derived from the proper application of knowledge and the other Keys to Winning that I just mentioned, and will now discuss in greater detail. These are the same principles that most of us apply on a daily basis in all our lives. When you see one store advertise peanut butter for $1.25 and another store advertise the very same product for 89¢, you go to the store where the price is better for the same product, right? That's *applying your knowledge to your financial benefit*. Those who buy the more pricey item either don't care about money or are losers without knowing it. So if you are in a casino, and you see some slots with a sign that says: "Up to 94.7 percent pay-back," and the casino next door has the same slots with a sign that says: "98 percent payback," where would *you* play? If you're a smart slot player who wants to win, you'd go to the one that says "98 percent payback," because you know that advertising which says "up to" doesn't mean that *all* the machines pay that much. You also know that 98 per-cent is better than 94.7 percent. Put those two together, and you have *made a knowledgeable decision* about where to play.

Yet so many people lose sight of these simple rules of everyday life when they visit a casino. They become blinded and forget to make their "shopping" choices work for them. As a result, many will lose and wonder why, and even more will wonder why they haven't had the kind of good play and fun as those other people for whom coins

keep falling into the tray, while they only feed the machines. Yes, slot machines are *machines*. They are preprogrammed to pay on certain pays, appear to run in certain
cycles, are set to pay back certain percentages, and so on
and on. Yet if no slot machine ever paid a jackpot, no one
would play them, and casinos as we know them wouldn't
exist. Therefore, to be a winner, and to win more often than
most people, you must apply your powers of *choice* and
combine this with the other Keys to Winning.

How do you acquire this knowledge? You've already
started. By reading this book and learning what is shown
here, you are on your way toward becoming an *informed*
player, and therefore a *better* player, whose luck is *cal-
culated* and not merely a blind act of good fortune. There
is a lot more to being a winner playing slots than many
people imagine. To most people the slot machine is merely
a simple device into which you stick some coins or currency, pull the handle or push the button, and then see if
you won something. Although this is the most basic principle of how slot machines function, there's much more you
should know when playing them. There is an old saying
that goes something like this: "Even a blind hog can find an
acorn once in a while." Simply put, this means that even if
you know nothing, every now and then, you will win. It
happens, and it happens frequently. I have seen people
come to Las Vegas who have never been to a casino, and
have never even seen a slot machine. They are flabber-
gasted, overwhelmed. Everything is new to them. Inno-
cently they walk up to one of the worst kinds of machines,
such as a Flip-It or the Big Bertha, drop in a few coins, and
presto! Here comes the jackpot! Unbelievable, right? Yes and
no. Sometimes even these people don't realize that they
have won something. All those bells ringing must mean
they broke the machine, and they try to leave. As odd as this
may sound, I have seen casino executives desperately trying

to convince such novice slot players not only that they did *not* break the machine, but that they actually won a big jackpot. Many such people are so "green" that they need such convincing. Of course, after they are convinced, the reality sets in, and all of a sudden they are slot players. From that point on they think winning at slots is easy, and they try again. And again. And again. And often, no such luck ever happens again for them.

Therein lies the greatest problem with slot players. They don't learn from their past experiences, or the experiences of others they have witnessed, known, or heard about. They remember that one time they were lucky, but not all the other times when they were *not* lucky. Most of all, they never realize that luck like theirs is like that blind hog finding that acorn. Once in a while such blind luck happens, but there are long "whiles" in between such happenings, and they may never happen to you again. Such people not only did not learn from their experience, they did not even know that any learning is necessary. And they did not pursue any such knowledge even after repeatedly trying to recapture that "luck."

Whenever such really novice players have a streak of luck, most casino people will explain to them not only that they have won, but that such a large win is extremely rare. Then they will usually refer them to some more information about gaming, and about the games provided in casinos. Even the most rudimentary information, such as that provided by most major casino resorts in the hotel rooms, is better than nothing at all. Although most of this information isn't exactly helpful, because it talks mainly about how to play the games that the casino happens to offer (and not necessarily about how to play these games *well*), nevertheless even this information is more knowledge than most novices have. Unfortunately, many people ignore even that little knowledge.

Although this example of the really "green" novice may be extreme, it serves to illustrate a wider problem among slot players. Even players who have been to casinos several times, who are now familiar with how slots work and may even possess some of that rudimentary knowledge from the in-room pamphlets or information obtained through conversations with other players—even these people do not necessarily behave, or play, in any more profitable manner than did those very "lucky" novices. Just because you have been to a casino and have played slots before, doesn't mean you know all you should know. Maybe you have won. Maybe you have lost. Perhaps you have won and lost, and are about even. What if you only lost a little? Does that make you feel comfortable about your casino slots expertise?

Being "comfortable" is an important concept. Many people feel uncomfortable at the beginning. Either because they are among those very "green" novices, or have only recently become more familiar with casinos, the casino environment, and the slot machines found there. As with most things we human beings do, there is what is called a "learning curve." This simply means the time it takes most of us to learn at least the very basics of whatever it is we are planning to do, or are doing. Once that is achieved, then there is another concept commonly known as the "comfort factor." This is the point we reach, eventually, after having done whatever we have contemplated through the learning curve process. We reach this point of the comfort factor when we have had direct experiences with that particular situation and found that we liked it, that it was good, that it was profitable, or that it didn't really hurt that much.

When we "like" something, usually it's because it does something for us which is pleasing, such as being entertained by the experience with the slot machine. Whenever we think that something was "good," this usually means that the entertaining experience we liked so much also proved rewarding in some way. This leads us to the part which we call "profitable," and although this normally means that we made some money, with slot machines this could be as simple as having received a pay. Any pay. Even a small pay which, in reality, meant an overall loss. But just the act of getting it, with the other factors combined, often results in our *perception* that this was "profitable," in which case we usually think of "profit" as something in addition to mere money. The casino experience, for example. Or the camaraderie among players. Or the fact that we were there with a loved one and shared a happy time, overall, which had little to do with the act of profiting from this particular slot machine. Maybe we reached the comfort factor after having lost money, but we got some play for it, and therefore the other factors in this human equation were satisfied, and consequently we thought about this as the "payment" for that series of experiences. Even though we lost money, we still feel okay about it because it "didn't hurt that much."

For most people, the loss of money is a hurtful experience. However, many people will become more resistant to that feeling after having played slots for a while. They quickly come to find out that the loss of money is an integral part of the playing experience. No one will win all the time. Losing is just as much a part of the playing of slot machines as is winning. And losing happens a lot more often than winning.

Once we all start to realize these human factors, we have entered the comfort zone, that point in our psychological approach to slot playing where we are no longer in wonderment about the game, and no longer in fear about the loss of our money. As a slot player, when you reach this point of familiarity with the game, and the comfort level regarding the experience, the money, the game, the winning and the casino environment, then you have developed what can be described as "casino familiarity," or perhaps "gaming resilience." You are no longer a novice, and the act of playing slot machines no longer scares you.

Now you have a decision to make, and a very important one. You can continue being happy with what you know, continue to play the machines with this minimal familiarity, and hope for the best. This will relegate you to the vast majority of casino slot players who have reached this point of familiarity with the game, and continue to try for the stroke of blind luck—like that hog still rummaging around hoping to find that elusive acorn. These are the slot players who feed billions of dollars into the casinos' coffers, and these are the people who are very largely responsible—to the tune of around 80 percent of all the casino revenue—for the cumulative huge losses suffered by casino slot players every year. If you really think about it, the numbers are staggering. In Nevada alone, casinos "win" over $9 billion each year. Yes, that's *billion.* Nine times one thousand millions. Of dollars!

Of this, some 80 percent comes from these slot players. This is a total cumulative loss of around $7.2 billion. In Las Vegas, the total casino "win" for a recent year was around $4.9 billion. That represents all the casinos in the Las Vegas area, about 100 or so casino resorts and casino hotels. Of this sum, again, about 80 percent was from slot players. This meant that these slot players cumulatively lost over $3.9 billion. Yes, of course these are rounded estimates based on reported information, but the example is quite valid, as are these actual numbers from published reports. There were around 36 million visitors to Las Vegas in that year. Of those, about 86 percent played slots. This means that from 30.1 million slot players, the *casinos won* a total of around $3.9 billion! Although the average loss was only about $157 for each of the 31,000,000 slot players, the truth is that not all of these people were playing only these amounts. The average bankroll for these visitors was around $670. Among those who said that they are gamblers, the average bankroll was closer to $1,200 for the "bring with you" money. On exit, it turns out that most of the players actually accessed additional funds which brought the average per-player "loss" to about $3,200.

The point of all this is to show you how easily the comfort factor translates into huge financial losses. As a consequence, if you continue to be happy with what you already know, or think you know, about the playing of slot machines, then you will be part of this great mass who lose that average amount each time they come. And notice also that this is an average *loss*, and not an average win. There's a big difference between them, in reality and in concept. The truth is that a smaller portion of these slot players will lose many millions, while the majority will lose a lot more than the few hundred, and a smaller portion will lose about the average, or less. But the fact remains that *they all lost*!

So the second decision you must make for yourself is whether you want to graduate from the comfort level and reach a point of expertise. This doesn't mean that you have to become a professional gambler. Although there are many books which suggest that's what you will have to do, that is far from the truth. To become an expert at playing slots doesn't mean you have to become a professional gambler, or even an author of gaming books. It simply means that you take the time to learn more than the average Joe, and give yourself the ability, and the knowledge not merely to lose what the average player loses, but to actually join the very elite club of players who win.

It *is* possible to win, you know. And no, you don't have to trust to blind luck, and you don't have to stumble around in the dark like that blind hog still looking for his acorn. People like me, who write books on gambling, are sort of like your seeing-eye dog. We lead the way. We point to the right things, and show how to do it the better way. This doesn't mean it is the only way, or even the right way. It simply means that from all our years of dedicated research, of playing, of living this life, we have acquired more than the average Joe's amount of knowledge, and are now able to apply it to suggestions and recommendations which we consider valuable. At least I do. Speaking for myself, I am writing this book, and the other books in this series, for the purpose of imparting to you the knowledge it took me more than two decades to accumulate. I am well aware that the learning curve can be difficult to overcome, while the comfort factor is easily reached. Therefore, I seek to simplify the information and make it as clear as I can, with as much impact as is possible to impart to it. By investing your time in reading this book, you have shown that you have the desire to improve yourself as a slot player, and reach a level of expertise.

It's not easy. Simplicity belies complexity. Slots aren't just odd little diversions. They are serious gambling games which can, and will, take your money if you don't know what to do, and how to do it to the best level the game allows. To learn this takes time and the willingness not just to learn it, but also to apply it, and apply it correctly. To help you do this, along with all the other information in this book, I have created the Keys to Winning. These are, in order of importance (as I see it), as follows:

1. Knowledge
2. Patience
3. Bankroll
4. Selection
5. Discipline
6. Win goal

Oh, how simple it seems when we just look at these simple words. Sure, you say. *No* problem. I can do that. Can you? Really? Be honest, now. I can tell you from direct personal experience that keeping yourself diligently to these principles is very, very hard to do. If, that is, you want to do this always, all the time, each time. To be a successful slot player, and win most of the time, you *must* keep to these principles. If you leave home to go to a casino, and you leave just one of these principles at home, or you slip and lose one, or more, or a part of one, you're sunk. You're the *Titanic* on a collision course with the iceberg, and there's no stopping the final result, or the consequences. And that's no joke. Believe me. I know. Not even I can be perfect at all times, and I don't expect you to be either. Just *most of the time.* There will be times when you will have the best intentions, but you will fail. You will leave home without one or more of these vital principles. And you will regret it. This I also know. I have done it, and so will you; count on it.

The point I am making is not that I expect you to become superhuman and suddenly be able to practice these principles with religious zeal, and equally perfect ability. That simply won't happen. Furthermore, any "system," or any advice you may read which says "do this and you will win," is fundamentally flawed, because no human being can be perfect at all times, each time, all the time. We are frail creatures, mentally, physically, and, most important, emotionally. We get upset. We get angry. We get mad that we have done everything perfectly, and still we lost. It happens. That's also part of life, and certainly part of the gaming experience. Even when you take all these principles with you, and do everything perfectly, even then there will be times when you will lose. This I also know from direct personal experience. These are those statistical anomalies which infect every aspect of gambling, and slots are certainly one of the games most prone to such visible fluctuations. Other games are equally prone, but these events are more hidden. Not so in slots, and that's why you will suffer, sometimes, even when you do it right.

My aim is to let you in on the "secret" which will allow you to overcome these problems, these feelings, and these moments of anger. That's why knowing these principles, as I have outlined them, is so important. Not because you will become perfect, or a professional gambler. But because *you will become more secure in your gaming*, more steady in your approach, more confident in your end result, and more conscious of your expectations. And these are the real secrets to your success playing slots. So, in more detail, I will now address each of those principles individually.

KNOWLEDGE

This should be relatively easy. This is the learning curve, the decision to improve yourself, and probably the reason you bought this book. Knowledge means to learn as much as possible, with the best possible direction toward your end goal. Knowledge means to know not just that slot machines exist, or what they look like and how to play them, but also how to play them *well*. Playing slots *well* also means incorporating into your knowledge all the other principles of these Keys to Winning. And it also means not stopping here. It means to include everything in this book and the others to which I refer. Knowledge is growth in understanding and in continual improvement. For slot machine play, this means everything I have written here, from page one to the last page. All of this knowledge is necessary to achieve more than just blind luck in your slot play. Acquiring it will have a direct and positive impact on your play and on your life, and specifically on how you approach the slot machines the next time you visit a casino.

PATIENCE

I am often surprised at how easily people get upset over slot machines. They get upset when they don't hit. They get upset when they do hit, but they don't think it's enough. They get upset if they don't hit the jackpot. When they hit a secondary jackpot, they get upset that they didn't hit the top jackpot. And when they hit the top jackpot, unless it's something in the millions, they get upset because they couldn't hit it sooner. Are you this kind of player? Does this fit your slot playing profile? If it does, then you aren't patient. You are hyper. You shouldn't play slots, at least not without a tranquilizer. Playing slots can be a very prolonged experience, one that will require your utmost patience. Slot wins will happen, and although sometimes you may be lucky and get that good win right away, most of the time it will not be that easy. You will have to work for it for a while. This may require you to do several sessions, and perhaps even visit several casinos. Maybe you will have to make several trips before you achieve that desired win goal. Setting achievable win goals is part of the art of patience.

I call it the "art" of patience because that's what it is. Patience is not a skill, and it is not a science. It is art. Skills can be learned. Science can be learned. But you must be born with the ability to be patient. You cannot learn to be that way. Fortunately, almost all human beings are born with that ability. The vast majority of us are born with the ability to learn languages, to deal with our environment through our senses, and to find out how to survive. These are all inherent abilities. We also have the ability to be patient. Unfortunately, the pace of our modern world rarely rewards patience, at least visibly. Although most achievements which we see publicly are the result of hard work and a lot of patience, by the time we see these achievements they have already happened. To us, they seem to have happened overnight. The old story among actors who finally gain star status goes something like this: "After thirty years of acting, suddenly I'm an overnight success." This is also true for many other disciplines. Take the making of a movie. First comes the idea. Then the story. Then the script. Then the producer. Then the studio. Then the money. Then the actors. Then the other details. Then the filming. Then the editing. Then the postproduction. Then the release. Although all of this is much more complex, the example works well for us here. By the time you get to see this film, most of the people involved in it have worked on it for several years. To you this looks as though the success just happened. To them, it's been a long grind, requiring lots and lots of patience. What about this book? It takes a long time to write a book like this. By the time you read these words, I will have spent two years writing. Even if the actual writing takes less time than that, publishers usually work on a schedule which is eighteen months in advance. This means that even if you were to write your own book, starting right now, the soonest you could expect to see it in print at the local bookstore would be two years from the first moment you wrote the first word. It takes enormous patience, including the fact that you often don't start to make money on it until three years later. Think about it. What if you went to your job this month, and your employer said: "Great work! Congratulations! We are very pleased. Your paycheck will be sent around June—three years from today." Would you have that patience? Would you be able to wait?

These examples are here to demonstrate that success playing slots is not merely that once-in-a-lifetime blind luck event. You can be successful as a slots player each time you play, overall throughout your career as a player of slots, but only if you develop your art of patience. Notice I said "develop," rather than "acquire." You already possess that ability, but like the ability to draw, you must practice and learn, and learn from doing, and learn from mistakes. It won't be easy, but then nothing worthwhile usually is. Developing patience means that you will curb your natural reactions. These are the emotional bursts, such as exuberance when you win, and anger when you lose. Both are the extremes along the scale upon which your slots success is measured.

The first trick to developing the art of patience when playing slots is to realize that great and glorious wins *will* happen and that equally great and horrendous *losses* will also happen. Both are the extremes along the scale of life's probabilities. The second trick is to develop the ability to curb your reactions to those extremes. Be happy when you win, but remember that it will not always happen. Remember that the money you *don't* lose back today will spend very nicely tomorrow, when you have a cooler head and a clearer perspective. When you lose, curb your reaction equally. Don't start to question yourself beyond reason. If you feel you have forgotten some part of your knowledge, by all means look it up. See if you were correct, and if not, learn from the experience. Even when you realize that you did everything correctly and still suffered that great and horrendous loss, curb your instinct to blame everything and everybody. Try not to destroy yourself or the solid foundations of your slot playing abilities. Remember that this is just the other end of the scale and that in this instance, the law of probability simply worked against you.

It may take what you consider a long time. The phrase "a long time" means to us, as human beings, something entirely different than to the universal event statistics. What you consider "a long time" may be only a tiny fraction of a microsecond in the overall scope of universal time. For example, I know a professional blackjack player who plays flawlessly every time, and always does everything correctly. He is in his twelfth year of a losing streak. I also know several professional poker players. One is in his sixth year of losing, and the other is in his eighteenth year of posting losses. Are those "a long time"?

It depends. The first poker player is starting to win. By the time you read this book, he will be in a positive curve.

The other poker player is playing smaller stakes now and has been on an upward swing, booking positive results again. My blackjack player friend gave up and moved out of town.

The point is that it's all relative. If you play slots for two hours and you don't reach your win goal, was that losing streak "a long time"? Well, for you, perhaps. But you should be conscious of the fact that the universe doesn't revolve around your particular perception of reality, or length of time. Patience, therefore, is the art of being able to react to each situation *without overreacting to it*—and that's where the greatest benefit lies. You will have to work this out yourself, because no person is identical to any other, and no two people deal with the same set of circumstances in exactly the same way. Therefore, no specific advice is possible. However, a plausible guideline to achieving patience *is* possible, and that's why I describe this in such detail. Patience will not only enable you to play slots better, but will also allow you to reach your comfort level far more quickly and with far more positive results. By realizing that patience is a requirement for enjoyment and profit from slot play, you will become far more at ease with the process. This will relax you under a variety of circumstances and situations, and will allow you to take a far more rational, and less emotional, approach to whatever these situations may be, or whatever action you may be required to undertake.

BANKROLL

All of these Keys to Winning are important, but Bankroll is perhaps the foremost. The reason is quite simple: Without money, you can't gamble. Gambling is all about money. Losing money and, of course, winning money. You must have it to start; you can't start without it. Even credit is money, and so is a credit line at the casino. It doesn't matter how you acquire your money, but whatever money you bring with you, or send to the casino cage, or get in credit at the casino constitutes your bankroll. This is the money you have designated as your gambling money. Your gambling stake. It should *not* be money you desperately need for your family's rent, mortgage, food, clothing, health care, and so on. This should be accumulated "spare" money, something you can afford to lose without such a loss having a devastating impact on you and your family. Any gambling bankroll should be made up of money you have designated as *expendable*. This doesn't mean that it should be treated as already lost, and hence treated recklessly. After all, it's still your money. You may have worked for it for a year or more and saved it up for your casino trip. Or you may have accumulated it through interest on investments, or from the sale of something you made or owned, and you don't need the overage for your survival. Remember that even though this money should be considered expendable, it is still important money and should be highly regarded. It was your work that made it possible. Just because you designate it as your gambling money doesn't mean it has suddenly lost its value. It still spends just the same.

Many people make the classic mistake of setting aside their gambling money with the conviction that it's already gone, dead, done, lost, and therefore means nothing. Wrong! This is a defeatist attitude. Thinking like this will result in two inevitable occurrences. First, if you have already convinced yourself that you are a loser, that you will lose, and therefore this money is already lost, you will gamble recklessly, without thought or regard to the value of the money, or the consequences of your reckless actions. As a result, you *will* lose, and this will reinforce your conviction that "Ah, well, it was already lost. I knew it." So you will be happy in your loss, because you convinced yourself that it was inevitable.

Second, you will not play knowledgeably, and certainly not in concert with these Keys to Winning. So, again, you will lose. When you do, this becomes yet another reinforcement of your initial starting attitude. "So," you now say to yourself, and quite possibly to anyone who will listen, "it was only gambling money. I knew I was gonna lose it, so what? It was my 'mad' money, anyway. Ah, well. Maybe next time." You have now thoroughly convinced yourself that you are a loser, and justified your initial defeatist attitude by making sure that you lost. If this is how you think, throw this book away, go buy a gun, put one bullet in the chamber, spin the chamber, put the gun to your head, and pull the trigger. You have a one-in-six chance that the first click will be a dud. You also have a one-in-six chance that the first click will be one you'll never hear. Either way, you are a loser, and that's it. This kind of an attitude has no place in life, and certainly none in gambling.

Your bankroll is your lifeline. It is essential. It should be protected and handled with care. In addition, it must be sufficient to carry the weight of your action. Think of this example: Say that you are about to take a bungee jump from one of those carnival bungee jump platforms. You weigh 200 pounds. Your bungee cord is your lifeline. If it breaks, you are history, toast, dead meat. Would you insist that the organizers of this jump give you a cord designed only to support a 150-pound person? I don't mean ask, I mean *insist*. Cause a ruckus. Absolutely *demand* that they give you the very cord which will break, and cause your downfall. Literally. Would you? Sounds insane? Inane? Yes, indeed. All of these and more. Yet this is precisely what the vast majority of all people who go to a casino do. Exactly that.

These people go to play slots with a bankroll which is far less than what is required even to start any kind of play on even the lowest-of-the-low slots. Not only that, these people take that meager bankroll and go for the big, expensive slots. They start with the $5 and $10 machines, or even higher. Or the ones that take 45 coins or 90 coins per pull. That's like going to the top of that bungee jump, then unhooking themselves from the bungee cord, and tying a short shoelace to themselves instead, then smiling at the people around them as they jump off the tower to their inevitable doom. As silly as this sounds, so many people are guilty of this that it is unfathomable how this can continue. Not only once, these people do this again and again. It becomes a self-defeating cycle for them, and they wonder why they "never seem to have enough" to win. Another catchphrase of the perennial loser.

Don't be like that. When you go to the casino, take enough money with you so that your starting bankroll is at least sufficient to support your expected action. Like the bungee cord, don't jump off if your action is designed for $200 and all you have is a $150 lifeline.

The amount of your bankroll should be determined by several factors. First, it depends on what this money means to you at that time. If this money is truly unencumbered, you will feel a lot better about making it a true bankroll. If this money is not completely unencumbered—such as when a portion of it should be used for something else, but that something else is not one of the essentials to survival—then maybe you will not handle the bankroll as well, or it may not be big enough. As a general rule, a gambling bankroll should be made up only of money which is entirely unencumbered. No part of it is needed, or could even be considered as being needed, for something else. Unencumbered money is free, and not scared. Encumbered money will always be scared money, and in gambling, scared money will fly away quickly. Playing with scared money means you are afraid to lose it. This doesn't mean that you have adopted the defeatist attitude we discussed earlier. It simply means that you have allocated at least some part of your bankroll either as an inadequate amount, or being encumbered upon something else—borrowed from a credit card, perhaps—which means you will have to pay it back, probably at great stress to you or your family. This is a very bad way to start your bankroll. Always start your bankroll with free money, which will become a solid gambling stake and not frightened at the prospect of being lost.

Second, the amount of your bankroll should be determined by the kind of machines you intend to play. If you want to play $5 reel slots, then your bankroll should reflect that. If you want to play higher limits than that, then your bankroll should be proportionally higher. If you plan to play $1 reel slots, or the video slots which may be nickels but require you to play $2.25 per spin (45 coins) or more, then your bankroll should adjust to that. In addition, whatever your intended action, your bankroll should be adequate to withstand fluctuations, not only in your fortunes as you play, but also in your decisions concerning the *kinds* of games you will play. For example, you may have decided to play $1 reel slots on this trip and allocated your bankroll for that action. But when you get to the casino, you discover that the kinds of machines you wanted to play are occupied, unavailable, or no longer there. Now what? Your bankroll should have a "slush" factor, allowing it to withstand the necessity for such on-the-spot decisions. What if you saw another kind of machine and decided to play that instead? Your bankroll should be adaptable to such deviations from your initial starting strategy.

So how do you arrive at the bankroll figure? Hard to say. It's different for each player. You know yourself and your circumstances. I don't know you or your circumstances. Therefore, all I can do is offer you *guidelines*, with the hope that you will have learned enough in this book so that you can intelligently adapt this guideline to your specific situation.

If you plan to play about three hours a day, for an average of three days, I can offer the following guidelines:

$1 reel slots =	$1,000 minimum
$5 reel slots =	$5,000 minimum
45-coin nickel video slots =	$500 minimum
90-coin nickel video slots =	$1,000 minimum
Quarter 3-coin reel slots =	$800 minimum
Quarter 2-coin reel slots =	$600 minimum
Progressives: $1 *three*-coin =	$100 for a tryout
	After that, play something else.
Progressives: $1 *two*-coin =	$80 for a tryout
	After that, play something else.
Progressives: quarter 3-coin =	$60 for a tryout
	After that, play something else.
Progressives: quarter 2-coin =	$40 for a tryout
	After that, play something else.

What does all this mean, and why is this so? Consider this: For the $1 reel slots, playing 3 hours a day for 3 days, this bankroll of $1,000 comes to only $333 per day, which is only $111 per hour. This is *barely* adequate. Personally, I wouldn't go near this kind of action without at least $3,000 as the starting bankroll. But most people will balk at these amounts, so I'm trying to make this at least feasible, and at the same time workable. The $1,000 bankroll is adequate; it will give you that average per-hour amusement, and it will give you a chance to win. However, the best way is to triple that bankroll. That amount will give you the the best odds of success. Again, these are only guidelines. I have no way of knowing what your personal situation may be, or how you see the requirements of a gambling bankroll.

For the $5 reel slots, the $5,000 minimum bankroll comes to $1,666 per day, and about $555 per hour. That's about as close to the bare minimum as you can get, but it is adequate. In $5 machines, $500 buys you a rack. Assuming 2 coins per pull, with an average of around 15 seconds per pull, plus another 5 seconds for various delays, such as credits running up on the meter, cocktail servers coming by, and so on, this will give you about 3 pulls per minute, which comes to total play time of 37 minutes. About right, for this kind of action. Enough time to enjoy the game, rack in the coins, cash in, and go find another machine for the second hour, and so on. Quite respectable. Personally, I would prefer a stake of $1,000 per hour, for $3,000 per 3-hour day, and a total of $9,000 for the 3-day trip, as defined. But that's up to you. This guideline is, again, derived from the base minimum of what you will need to give the game the best chance to pay you.

Those video nickel machines are a toss-up. With 45 coins, that is $2.25 per pull. With 90 coins, that is $4.50 per pull. Adjust the above figures for the $1 and $5 reel slots, and you can come up with a median on your own.

The quarter reel slots are, well, a downer. I'd say don't play them at all. But if you must, then bring at least that amount of money. It won't be the most interesting experience you ever had, but perhaps you are new to slots, and this will give you at least a reasonable introduction to the slot playing experience. But try to graduate from the quarter reel slots, and reach at least the $1 level. It will be far more rewarding, and only a little more expensive.

Finally, the progressives. Most of the progressives have enormous odds against a win. Some are no better than state lotteries, with odds of hundreds of millions to one against you. If you must try them, allocate 5 percent of your bankroll, or no more than $100 for those that take $1 tokens (usually 3 at a time), or no more than $40 to $80 for those which are quarters, or nickel progressives. That's it. That's your experience with progressives. If you are really lucky and win millions, so much the better, because it didn't cost you thousands, or tens of thousands, to get it. Be thankful, and send me a commission. For the rest of us, well, we enjoyed our few dollars in the progressives, won nothing, but at least we tried. So now we will do what we know is better—allocate our bankroll for better uses and play those machines which are a much better investment for our hard-earned gambling bankroll.

SELECTION

This is the part where "skill" in slot play comes into the picture. Many people believe that winning at slots depends purely on luck. While it is correct that slots are a passive game and, therefore, you cannot control the outcome of the event, it is not correct to say that playing slots involves no skills. I don't mean merely the skills of being able to operate the machine that contains the game. I am referring to skills such as game selection, machine selection, brand name selection, game detail selection, size of wager selection, payout hierarchy selection, credit vs. coin play selection, play methodology selection, size of bankroll selection, play duration selection, time to play selection, casino to play in and what kinds of machines to play there selection, and the remaining variety of various applied skills which you will acquire as you continue reading this book, and then put your own abilities into practice. There is a lot more to being a winning slot player than just showing up at the casino, sticking your money in the machine, and pulling the handle.

Each of these skills is part of the learning curve and comfort zone which all of us have to reach. By acquiring these skills, you can become not only more knowledgeable, but also more comfortable. You will find that you are no longer a victim to the mere chance of luckily selecting just the right machine, at the right time, and for the right reasons. You will now be able to approach your casino visit with the ability to look for and select the kinds of games which you know are among the better options, and do so with a solid plan of attack. Not only will this result in more confidence and comfort for you when you play, but it will directly translate to regular profits. Although you won't win every time, or perhaps achieve your win goal every time you play, you will now be able to realize that this is a part of the overall approach to the game. You will no longer be a victim to emotional swings, such as deep disappointment when you don't win or reckless exuberance when you do. Although curbing these emotional reactions is part of Patience, as discussed above, and also Discipline, discussed below, the selection skills will contribute to your overall Keys to Winning. The slot machines will no longer hold the "secret" but will divulge it to you, because you now know what to look for, and how to do it to your best advantage.

Now let's take a look at some of the selection skills in more detail. Remember that each is part of an overall whole, and even though each is important, the sum of the whole is far more crucial to your winning success at playing slots than any single part. Often you will have to make adjustments, even while you are playing, because in the real world not all of these skills will apply all the time. Neither will all of the advice I am offering here, nor the guidelines. However, all this information, viewed together, forms the greater whole, and this is the sum total of what will eventually become your slot playing expertise.

Game Selection

This very important skill can be acquired through the Knowledge part of these Keys to Winning. Notice that while Patience was an "art," these are "skills." Anyone can learn these skills. All it takes is the desire to be a winner, the ability to understand the information being offered, and the ability to apply that knowledge to gaming success.

Game selection includes several items. What kind of machine? Reel slots, video slots, video poker, other kinds of slots? In which denomination? What kind of game? As with all these skills, the answers to these questions are all part of the overall picture. Your success in playing slots depends on all of these abilities. Such answers will be supplied by yourself. The kind of machine, game, and denomination may be determined by your bankroll, interest, and win goal. Other factors will influence how you approach the other skills of game selection. Generally, you should select a machine that is easy to play and understand, and one that takes 2 coins maximum (reel slots), or can be played for the minimum per-line investment (such as 9 coins in a nine-line video slot machine), without penalty or disadvantage to your win expectation and potential jackpot and bonus awards. This is the simplest and best advice to get you started. From this point on, your skills will dictate further advancements in your play.

Machine Selection

Often machines and their games can be one and the same, but some machines may have more than one game, such as multi-game video slots. Even simple single-game reel slots may have different games inside the cabinets. These games may look the same as the ones you have decided to select, but may not be. The easiest example is among reel slots which offer standard pays with the use of "double" symbols. There are many such games. Often, these games also have similar-looking symbols, but if you look closely you will notice that these are only "wild" symbols, and not the "double-up" symbols I mentioned earlier. This is also found quite frequently among similar-looking machines which may have the "double" symbols, but on one machine they also substitute for all the other symbols, as well as double the pay, while on the other machine they may only double that pay, but not act as substitutes for other symbols. Even though these machines look absolutely identical, this is a profound difference. On the one where these "double" symbols also substitute, the pays are far more frequent and in higher values. On the other machine, where these same symbols only double but do not substitute, the pays are far less frequent and their combined value is, therefore, less.

You will find reel slots like this everywhere. This is also true of video poker games, where two identical-looking machines can have extremely different pay and play programs. Such subtle differences can be more easily seen in video poker games, and also in some reel slot games, while being much more cleverly hidden in many video slot games. Some of the video reel slots have so many pays, and combinations of pays and bonuses, that it becomes very difficult to find out exactly how these games may be different from each other. The easiest clue I can give you is to look at the top jackpot amount. For example, many of these games will show the top jackpot as 25,000 coins. The exact and identical-looking machine, either elsewhere in the same casino or in another casino, may show that very same jackpot as 12,500 coins. Big difference. What does this mean? It means that at the game which offers only the 12,500-coin jackpot, you are getting less for the same risk, all other items being equal.

Often when you see this, you will notice that the other pays on the machine don't pay exactly as much, or in the same manner, as the machine with the bigger jackpot. Usually these differences in the top jackpot amounts are a good indicator that the game is just a bit different. The most glaring of these differences is, of course, in the top award. However, many times you will also find that the winning combinations among the rest of the pays aren't paying the same as the other game, even when everything looks the same. Often the difference may be as simple as the game paying only left to right, while the other, better game paid both ways. Or this game may only be a five-line game, while the other was a nine-line game. Or the bonus entry structure is less frequent because the requirements aren't set to occur as often as in the other game. Or some of the pay symbols, or bonus awards or rounds, may be missing.

There are a host of such subtle differences among these games. It is consequently very important that your machine selection also include comparisons. This will require a little legwork on your part, and some skills in observation. Among reel slots, this will be easier and faster, because you will not have to look much beyond the belly glass of the game to find out what kind of symbols it has, and what they do. Among the video slots, you will have to do more investigating. You will need to read the help and pay screens, learn the payoff and bonus structure and amounts, and then compare these to other machines of their kind, and especially to other machines that look the same. You can usually save yourself some time by first looking at the top jackpot amounts, which should give you an indication of the differences in the machine's pay and bonus structure. But there will be no substitute for diligence and ability to apply the skills and knowledge you have acquired. Your success as a slot player will, therefore, directly depend on your abilities to do these things.

Brand Name Selection

This is closely tied in with the above item. Machine and game selections are often influenced by the *manufacturer* of the game and machine. It's the same principle as the one you may be familiar with from shopping at the market or discount store. For example, you may plan to buy a certain kind of peanut butter, but you see a generic or store brand instead, and buy that. It looks the same. It spreads the same. But it doesn't quite taste the same. What's the difference? Well, the most immediately apparent difference was the price. You probably saved a few cents by buying that store brand. You read the label on both jars of peanut butter, and the list of ingredients was the same. They may both say "contains whole crushed peanuts," but the product you bought, for those few cents less, just doesn't taste right. Most often the reason for this is—as far as peanut butter is concerned—that the *quality* of the peanuts is different. Like anything which grows, there are levels of quality. These levels of quality extend not just to the original peanut, but also where it was grown, what were the soil conditions, how often was it necessary to "medicate" the plant by spraying it with pesticides, growth additives, and so on. Then, how well was it roasted, ground, and prepared? How long has it been since it was bottled and shipped? And so on. All of this influences the final taste of this product. So while the brand name product may have consistency in quality, and hence taste, the generic or store products may vary widely in quality and taste, because they may use ingredients from a wide variety of sources, regions, and quality. This doesn't mean that such generic products are always bad. Not at all. Many are just as good, if not better, than their counterparts. This example simply means that, sometimes, *based on your personal knowledge and experience,* it is more profitable to look at the brand name first, and then compare the other similar products to that standard.

Among slot machines, this is similarly so. There are some very well established brand names among manufacturers of slot machines. In this book, I have identified those which I consider to be the best and therefore the standard by which you can judge any slot machine, its performance, its pay program, and its potential for your profitable play. One of the secrets of successful slot play is the acquisition of knowledge regarding slot machine manufacturers and their products. Then you will be able to begin your machine and game selection by first identifying the brand names of the machines and games. Once you have done that, you will gain the standard by which to compare the other games on the casino floor. There will be many machines and many games. Some of them will look the same, or be very similar to the brand name, like that peanut butter example above, but may not play or pay quite as well. By simply being able to recognize the brand name of the machine or game, you will be well on your way to making intelligent and informed decisions.

Game Detail Selection

As with all of these items concerning selection, they are intertwined at many levels. "Game detail selection" refers to the small nuances in the game, the often hard-to-see differences in pays or in the way the games play. Among reel slots, this is not nearly as important as it is among the newest video slots. Reel slots tend to be much simpler and have very few details concerning their play and pays. While it is true that some of the reel slots can look very imposing and complicated, upon closer investigation you will soon discover that the basic game is usually very simple. It is the various bonuses, or the additions of other events (as in hybrid reel slots) that cause confusion. Also the preponderance of various symbols. The game detail selection for reel slots applies to your ability to identify and understand the pay and play structure of the game. Remember that the simpler it is, the better it is from the perspective of providing you with the best chance to win money. The more complex reel slots, or those offering a wider variety of symbols and various bonuses, may be more entertaining to play, but they will only rarely be as profitable as the much simpler reel slots which you can still find in most casinos.

For video slots, this is a little more complicated. Here the game detail selection is a far more precise science. Your abilities in this area directly influence your odds of success when playing these machines. It is imperative that you first learn everything about any video slot machine or game that you are contemplating playing. The machines offer this information among their pay, play, and help screens. Take the time to read all of this, and to understand it. Don't start playing until you know what pays what and under what circumstances, how it is done, what needs to be activated to do this, how many coins must be played to get the best payoffs and bonuses, and so on. It's also important to find out whether this is a "doubler" machine or a "buy-a-pay" machine. These are the "details" in your game selection.

Size of Wager Selection

This item is a companion to game detail selection. Once you have identified the details of what this machine is, and how it plays and pays, your next step is to decide how much you will invest. This is part of your bankroll decisions, but in this case we assume you have already settled on your bankroll for this game and now are simply judging how much to invest and how many coins, or lines, you will play.

For the reel slots, this should be easy. If it's not a 2-coin machine, with simple double-up symbols that also substitute for the other symbols, you don't play it. If it is a different kind of reel slot machine, and you have determined from the Top-10 list and the other information presented here that this machine is still a viable candidate for your investment, then *you* must judge the kind of play which you will give it. If it's a straight "doubler" machine, maybe you only want to play 1 coin. If it's a "buy-a-pay" machine, then you

will *always* play maximum coins. And so on, for whatever
the required decision may be, based on your skills of applying the knowledge you have acquired.

Among video slots, this selection principle is more complicated. First, you must learn the details. Once you have
done this, and now understand exactly what this machine
is, and how it plays and pays, then you can decide how
many coins you intend to play. Your first decision should
involve the number of available paylines. If the machine has
five lines, then the absolute minimum must be 5 coins. If it
has nine lines, then this is 9 coins. And so on. This should
be automatic for any such video reel slot machine. *None* of
these should be played with any *less* than the minimum 1
coin *per payline*. At least. Without this absolutely minimum
action, you will be a loser no matter what you have learned.
If you even think about playing such video reel slots for any
less than this absolute minimum, then you have not learned
very much. Yet. But you will. You will learn this two ways.
One is the easy way, and that is to follow this advice, from
the information gained here. The other is to play this way
and realize that you have won, but didn't get paid because
you didn't play at least that minimum of 1 coin per payline.
Once you do this, you won't ever forget it, and it will haunt
you the rest of your life.

Not so long ago a woman was playing a nickel slot machine, which happened to have a jackpot of $500,000. It was
a 3-coin machine, but she insisted on playing only 1 coin.
Well, you guessed it. She hit the Big One. Oh, but she only
bet 5¢. She won $50. For that extra 10¢, she would have had
half a million dollars. Stories like this are many. Is it sad?
Well, no. That player was just plain ignorant. There's no
excuse for this, or anything like this, particularly with these
multi-line video reel slots, where playing anything less than
the minimum bet which activates *all* the paylines is equally

ill-advised as was that woman who only played the nickel and didn't get the big pay when she hit it.

Consequently, it is essential that whenever you play any of these multi-line video slots, you play *at the very least* the minimum 1 coin *per payline* to activate *all* the paylines. However, your decisions do not end there. In addition, you should determine whether you should play the *maximum* coins or not. This will depend on all the other information about the machine and the game. All of this information becomes necessary when you make a decision that will cost you money. Some of these machines should *never be played for less than the maximum coins allowed*. This is because on these machines, you "buy-a-pay," and therefore if you play any less than the maximum bet, you will not get the best bonuses, the best pays, the jackpots, and will not get the best payback percentage of which such a machine is capable by its play program. On other machines, which may look similar, or actually look the same, the best way to play them may be by the mere 1 coin per payline, because these machines do not offer the "extras" for maximum coin play. You have to find this out for yourself, and then judge your wager selections accordingly.

As a simple rule to follow, *always play maximum coins*. If you can't afford to play maximum coins, don't play until you *can* afford to do so. Otherwise, you are throwing your money away, because you will never force the casino to pay you the amounts to which you are entitled by the machine's pay program. In all honesty, this should be automatic, and your decision already made up. However, there are times when skilled decisions can make a difference—decisions that require extensive knowledge of the game. In the end, that will be your decision, based on the abilities and skills you acquire through the information in this book, and your own abilities and playing successes.

Payout Hierarchy Selection

Your wager selection will be influenced by the payout hierarchy. This is the part on the machines which shows the graduated scale of payments, and bonuses offered. This information is usually found under the "pays" menu icon on video reel slots, and on the belly glass of reel slots. It tells you what amounts the game pays, how and when, and with what combinations. Further, it shows you whether this is a "doubler" or a "buy-a-pay" machine or game.

Some of these machines and games may look the same but have a different payout hierarchy. This we have already discussed. Don't forget to look at this payout hierarchy and make sure that you understand what it means and how it will affect your bankroll, your play and session investment, and your win expectation. You acquire this understanding by combining all of the information shown here and applying it to your *overall* machine or game selection.

Credit vs. Coin Play Selection

The vast majority of all slot machines, whether reel or video, will have credit meters upon which winning credits accumulate, and from which coins-per-play are deducted. There may still be some very old machines that take only coins, have no credit meter, and dump all wins into the coin tray, but these are most likely in a museum or perhaps part of personal collections. No modern U.S. casino of which I am aware still uses these old-style machines. So for the sake of all examples and further discussions, all machines to which I refer throughout this entire book will be the kind that have a credit meter.

The credit meter functions in two ways. First, if you insert paper currency the bill acceptor will read the value of that currency, and then credit to the credit meter the equivalent amount of that currency. So if you are playing a $1 reel slot machine and insert a $100 bill, then the credit meter will show 100 credits. The second function is to accumulate your wins. Continuing with this example, if you played the first pull at 2 coins, your credits would now have been reduced by those 2 credits, and so you would now have only 98 credits on the meter. But let us say that your first spin was a winner of 10 coins. The credit meter runs up and registers that win, and now you have 108 credits on the meter.

This is very convenient. I like credit meters, and also ticket printers on cash-out, because they avoid the need to deal with all those heavy and dirty coins, as well as fill delays, coin jams, and so on. For video slots, such credit play is absolutely essential. None of the modern video slots would be possible without credit meters and currency acceptors. Could you imagine yourself having to stuff 90 nickels, one at a time, into a tiny nickel-sized coin slot for each and every pull? You'd go nuts. The convenience factor of credit play has made the multi-line video slot games possible.

Among reel slots, this is less of an issue. Most of the better reel slots are in the $1 and $5 denominations, and since you should mostly play no more than 2 coins per pull (on 2-coin-maximum-wager machines, more on machines which require more coins for maximum play value), the credit play option does not have nearly the impact that it has for the nickel video slots, or the quarter video slots, where the requirement of multi-coin multi-line play is essential for the game and the win success. It is, however, very handy for keeping track of your progress as you play the machine.

Your choices are not too difficult. When playing any video reel slot machine, always use the credit play. Insert your currency, and then use the credit play from that point on. However, when playing *reel* slots, the opposite is better. Whenever possible, buy the number of coins you want first.

For example, if you intend to play a 2-coin reel slot machine in the $1 denomination, and you have selected $100 as your game session stake, then buy $100 worth of the $1 tokens from the change person or the change booth. Then play them in the machine as you intended, 2 coins per pull. Whatever wins you get will accumulate on the credit meter. Don't play those credits. They will provide you with a perfect gauge as to how well this machine is performing. At the end of your session, after you have run all the 100 coins through the machine, look at the credit meter and see what you have. It will then be easy for you to see exactly how well your machine did for this play session. You can then make further decisions accordingly. These are the two best ways to approach the coin vs. credit selection.

Play Methodology Selection

This has a lot to do with the kind of playing strategy and discipline which you will employ in your gaming. Learning information and acquiring the abilities and skills required to properly apply that information to your playing success are all necessary prerequisites. Eventually, you will also have to include a playing strategy, often referred to as the "overall methodology," meaning the approach you take to your play. Selecting the correct play methodology is more tricky. Not all methods, often called "systems," are appropriate for all machines, games, or occasions. Much of this is also dependent on your bankroll and on your win goals.

The best way to approach the selection of any methodology of play, is first to decide what kind of a machine or game you will be playing, the amount of your bankroll, and the number and frequency of your playing sessions. Once you have decided this, you can search through available strategies to determine the best one to use for this specific occasion. In Part Five of this book, I present some of the simplest and most easily applied strategies for profitable slot play, but this does not mean that you can't use your own strategy, or those which you may have learned elsewhere. Many of these strategies contain strong and applicable methodology, as it applies to particular games or machine situations. In the end, the decision will be yours to make. For now, the methods I offer here will empower you to start playing immediately and, later, to enhance your play according to your abilities and growing skills.

Size of Bankroll Selection

This is again dependent on a number of other factors. Simply put, the best way to gauge the size of your playing bankroll is to determine how much of your money you can afford to risk, without its loss affecting your ability to continue living at your present rate of comfort. If you think that a loss of $500 won't affect your ability to pay the rent, or the mortgage, or the power bills, and so on, then this is the bankroll you should take, and modify your play and win goals, accordingly. For higher amounts, this will depend directly on the value of that money to you at the time you are making this determination.

Never play slots, or any gambling game, with money you cannot afford to lose!

If you do this just once, you will think it's okay to do it again. It's *never* okay to do it. Playing this way means you are using "scared" money because the total loss of it will adversely affect you, your family, and your life. This is a prescription for disaster. Stories about people like this abound. Let's use this one, which I heard from a friend of mine.

A man who was considered the pillar of his community, a dedicated husband and father to two children, a steady employee who had been with the same firm all of his twenty-five years of work life, finally took the early retirement option offered by his company. Along with this, he received a sizable retirement benefit payment. Combined with this amount, and the fact that he owned his home, his car, and retirement investments which had mushroomed to a good amount, his children grown and with lives of their own, this man and his wife were the ideal middle-aged couple. Comfortably off. Neither would ever have to worry about money. For the rest of their lives, they could live comfortably, travel, enjoy themselves, take pride in their lives and in their children and, eventually, grandchildren. Life looked about as good as any poster could present.

One day, as they were considering what to do that spring, they decided to visit a casino. Neither had ever been to a casino before. They had rarely gone anywhere, having spent their lives working and raising a family. So, they thought, why not? Off they went. Neither knew anything about gambling, casino games, or slot machines. For the first few days, they had a great time. They went sightseeing, enjoyed the fine dining, the shows, and even played a little here and there. The wife didn't like it much, though, so they had decided to go back home earlier than they had planned. On the last night, the man went to play a slot machine one last time. He put in a few coins, pulled the handle, and won a $250,000 jackpot. Wow! He and his wife were overjoyed. They planned to spend the money on their children, buy them each a house, invest some money for their expected grandchildren's education, and so on. They packed up and went home with all that money.

About two years went by. Then one day the local newspaper reported that the man had been arrested for trying to rob the local bank, where he and his family had banked all their lives. Not only was this a stupid act, since everyone in the town knew these people, especially at the bank, but as the investigation proceeded, it revealed that this man was far from the pillar of the community he had pretended to be. Much to the surprise of everyone, particularly his wife and children, he was in debt to several casinos for over $2 million. It seems that shortly after he won that $250,000 jackpot, he had started to play slots regularly. He apparently hid these trips from his wife by claiming to have taken a part-time job in the travel business, which required him to do some destination traveling. He went back to that same casino. His initial success was reinforced again when he was lucky the second time and won another $50,000. From this point on, he convinced himself that he was a great gambler, and that this would be the easiest money he would ever make for himself and his family.

So for the next two years, he became a regular visitor to that casino and others in the area. Soon he was known as a high roller and was given lots of perks, comps, freebies, gifts, and so on. He thought he was the king of slots. But he wasn't winning any more. Instead of *learning something* about the casino games, he began to play bigger amounts and more often. Within months of his two big wins, he had lost all of it back to the casino. Then he started to dip into his savings and retirement money. Soon the casino, and other casinos, started to offer him large lines of credit, not knowing that he was now playing with money he couldn't afford to lose. As careful as casinos are not to extend credit to people who may be in trouble, there was simply no way for anyone to know. And so he gambled, and lost. And kept losing. He never won anything again, but he was still convinced that he was a great player, and that if he only bet more, bigger, and more often, he would recover the money he lost, and the money he borrowed, and everything would be fine. It wasn't. Two years after those great casino wins, he was not only flat broke, but had spent all of his retirement money, his retirement bonus, mortgaged the house and all their property, sold all the jewelry and assets, ran up all their credit cards and lines of credit and loans, and was in hock to the casinos for $2 million on top of that. In desperation, he tried to rob the only bank he knew. He was familiar with the bank, so he was convinced that robbing it would be easy. He was caught in the parking lot, tossing the bags of stolen money into his car. He is now in prison. His wife lives with her children—six months with one, and six with the other. They lost the family home. All their social security income and pensions are levied against debts, with only that portion allowed under law paid to them to live on.

What is the point of this very sad story? To remind you to *select your bankroll carefully*. The size of your gambling bankroll should always reflect your ability to survive its total loss.

Individually, for each machine or game you select, the size of your bankroll should be called your *session* bankroll. This is the part of your overall bankroll which you will allocate to this one machine or game, on this particular playing session, this one time. Such an allocation should reflect the overall size of your casino bankroll, divided into the session stakes according to the game of your choice, the time you wish to play, and the win goals you desire to achieve. I provided a framework for this strategy in the section about Bankroll. Please look it up and read it again in light of this additional information. It will help. Believe me, I know.

Play Duration Selection

Similar to the bankroll selection, the duration of your play on a particular machine or game should be governed by the amount of money you have allocated to this session, and your ability to physically sustain the play effort. If you get bored, stop. Being bored means you have lost interest in this game, and if you keep playing you will waste your money and your time, because you will not play the game correctly and will easily lose sight of your win goals. It's a trap. Be aware of it. Playing slots, particularly reel slots, can often get boring, especially when you play for several hours at a time. If your attention span is short and you get tired easily, or upset, or feel any kind of a negative emotion, then plan your play duration in short bursts. How short? Well, that depends on you. Personally, I can sit at a reel slot for hours on end and never get bored, as long as I have the starting mindset that I have a certain goal, and that includes the amount of time at the game. Other times, I decide that short sessions will be better because my personal psyche at that moment demands quick bursts to sustain the interest. We are all different, and you will need to choose according to your own particular situation, personally, financially, psychologically, and emotionally.

Never play any slot machine past the point where it continues to interest you.

If you have properly identified your goals and win objectives, then you should be psychologically prepared for as long as it takes, under the circumstances of your available casino time. If at any time you lose this conviction, and you lose interest in the game, that is a warning sign. Your mind and body are telling you that you have set goals beyond your ability, either mentally or physically. Listen to these hints. They will save you money. Therefore, your time-at-the-game selection requires you also to be honest with yourself, and not to set periods of time at play which you can't handle. If you don't know you have these limitations, and you find that out while playing, listen to what your mind and body are telling you. Many people don't realize that they have limitations; they get overly excited in the casino and lose their perspective on themselves and their lives, which usually means they lose their money as well.

Once in a casino, maintain your rational approach to slot play. Remember that any activity requires mental and physical exertion. Playing slots is no different. It will take time, effort, and concentration. Once you lose any of these three, or start to feel not quite committed, stop. Take a break. Go eat. Go take a swim, a spa, a massage. Sleep. Sit in the lounge. See a show. Whatever. You may need only a short break, perhaps just a few minutes. When I start to feel this way, I go to the rest room, wash my face, walk around the casino, maybe walk outside for a few breaths of fresh air, and I'm set to go again, refreshed and able to concentrate. This is very important. After you have been to a casino a few times and have practiced this advice, you will easily see just how important it is to your gaming success. Don't let your play of the slot machine control you. *You* control your time at this play. The game will reward you for it.

When to Play Selection

This will be affected by your general lifestyle. Most people get up in the morning to go to work at 9:00 A.M., come back after 5:00 P.M., then have dinner, and so on, and so to bed. This schedule defines the kind of lifestyle they lead. Coming to a casino, most people entirely forget this and start to act as if there were no need to sleep, rest, or do anything other than indulge in total abandonment. That is okay, believe me. There's nothing better than to become that free. For a while, that is, and without losing your head, and your money, while doing it. Unfortunately, many people get so wrapped up in this sudden freedom that they forget their rational mind. That is bad. If you want to have this "mad time," it is perfectly okay to do so. Just be aware that it will cost you money, and that it can cost you your well-made plans as well. Once you interrupt your routine, you will become trapped in paradise, and you can easily lose sight of even the most basic human reason. If this happens to you,

you are lost, at least for the duration of this trip. But fear not. It can be overcome.

When you plan your trip to the casino, regardless of whether you happen to live next door to the casino or have to plan a vacation to fly or drive there, remember that you will become enthusiastically enthralled in the experience. Plan for it. Plan for the mad time, and that way you will be able to allocate time, resources, energy, and bankroll to these experiences. Make that part of your casino plan, and you will have a great time enjoying it. Then, when you tire yourself out, remind yourself that it's time to get rest, regain your composure and reason, because now it will be time to go and play to win. Playing to win requires a clear head and a rested body.

You will need to make some adjustments to your normal lifestyle and schedule. Playing slots to win may require you to play at odd hours, because that's where the pickings are good. For example, most people tend to crowd around the slots at dinner time, and just after. Bad time. Everyone plays then, and the selections are few and far between. If possible, play either very late at night, such as after midnight, or very early in the morning, such as from about 5:00 A.M. The best time to play slots is usually from about 3:00 A.M. until about 9:00 A.M. This is the time in between the end of the rush from the night before, and prior to the rush from the "normal" morning risers, who play before and after breakfast.

There are very good reasons for this kind of play. First, there will be fewer players. You will have better choices among the machines and therefore be able to make better selections. You will also get better service from the employees, because there are fewer people for them to look after. Second, the machines you will select are quite likely to have been given a lot of play the night before, and therefore will be more primed for your skilled selections and play. In fact, if you want to do this and can handle it physically, stay up for some hours during the busy times the night before and watch the machines you think you will want to play. Don't play, just watch. See which machines get the heaviest play and what, if anything, they have paid out. This kind of prior research can serve you well when you rise early the next morning and hit the machines before the day crowd hustles in. Of course, you may want to go to bed early so you *can* get up early. Fine. You can still get the information you want, by asking the employees. They may not know for sure, because they have just come on duty after the swing shift leaves at 2:00 A.M., but I can assure you that if there was any kind of a significant win on the previous shift, these people in that area will have heard about it. Although this is nothing more than some simple empirical research, and is only useful as a guideline, and just one more piece in the overall informational supply, it still provides a good gauge by which to modify your game selections.

As a general rule of thumb, try to play slots whenever other people are not playing. Stay away from crowds and times when machines are crowded. That's not the time to play. That's the time to watch and learn and remember.

Casinos to Play In and What Kinds of Machines to Play There Selection

A long title, and not very grammatical, but pertinent. Which casinos to play in? Well, if you live near one or two and that's it, then your choices are simple, provided these are the casinos you want to visit. As a general rule of thumb, in the United States the best casinos for playing slots are in Las Vegas, Nevada. Machines in the state of Nevada are usually much better than they are in any other state, and those in Las Vegas are the best of any slots anywhere. On the East Coast, machines in Connecticut are better than machines in Atlantic City. If you want to know which casinos in the Midwest offer the better games—and yes, there are casinos even in the Midwest which have some very good slots—I refer you to *Midwest Gaming and Travel* magazine, published in Waseca, Minnesota. You can look it up on the Web, under the same name, all together, lowercase characters, and then the dot-com, of course. But overall, nothing can beat the slots in Las Vegas. They are the best, loosest machines anywhere. And the best variety of slots is found there, as well as most of the newest games.

DISCIPLINE

Of all the above Keys to Winning, this one sounds the simplest, but is the hardest of all. We all understand the value of discipline, especially when it comes to our money. This is accentuated when we talk about the casino environment. Everything in the casino is designed to separate us from any sense of reality. The casinos are a wondrous land where everything seems possible, as long as you still have money. Money is the lifeblood of all of this excitement. Without it, you are nothing more than dead wood, and you will be flushed out in a hurry. Having discipline as part of your winning objectives saves you from the inglorious fate of being washed clean, hung out to dry, and tossed away as yet another of the ill-prepared and unwary.

Having discipline as part of your tricks of the trade when you go gambling simply means that you make a commitment to play wisely, with reason, with goals in mind, and with all of the empowering information and Keys to Winning that I have shared here. If you want to have your mad time, that's okay too. Budget for it, realize it, recognize it, make it part of your overall game plan. Even that will then become part of your discipline. Just don't let the thrill of this overwhelm you or allow it to completely drown all your plans and your discipline along with it.

Unfortunately, *making* a commitment to self-discipline when going to the casino is very easy. *Keeping to it* once you get to the casino is very hard. So hard, in fact, that the vast majority of people who arrive at the casino completely convinced they will not allow this experience to get the better of them do just that. They let it get the better of them. And fast. You'd be surprised. Very often as soon as they walk through the door. Suddenly, they see all the excitement, all the games, all the flashing lights, the sounds of money and chips—the entire atmosphere captivates them. In the door they go, and out the door go all of their well-meaning and carefully conceived plans, their sense of discipline, and all their other senses as well. It happens to just about everyone, even hardened veterans of the casino lifestyle. All of us are human beings, and we are not perfect. We have failures, and lack of discipline is the worst. We see it everywhere around us. Schools no longer teach discipline. Rowdy and disruptive students are no longer punished. They are "counseled" instead. Same with children. The outcome is that we are producing a society where none of the adults have any idea of what discipline is. When they are faced with it, as when they enter the workforce, or the armed services, they are in complete shock. No wonder, then, that most people who go to casinos can't understand what discipline really is, and how it applies to their gaming success or financial failure.

To offer the easiest guideline, discipline in gambling simply means to remain conscious of the value of your money and conscious of your desired goals and objectives. It means, mostly, not to allow yourself to be drawn into the very comfortable, but financially deadly, "why not, it's only money?" syndrome. Once you have experienced the casino lifestyle a few times, you will often hear many people say things like that. These people, trapped in the losses they have incurred, are now trying to rationalize. They don't actually expect anyone else to be listening to them, or to really understand what expressions such as this really mean. They have just resigned themselves to the loss of all their money, and to the "I no longer care" attitude. That's the danger sign. Once you stop caring about the value of the money you are using to play—or are winning—then you have lost the discipline which comes with realizing that this money isn't just coins, tokens, or gaming chips. This money actually spends, the same as it does when you are buying food, gas for your car, paying bills, and so on. It is real money, and it has real meaning. Discipline means to remember this, and play accordingly.

This doesn't mean that you must be, or should be, a miser. Playing too carefully is also a prescription for disaster. I have already mentioned that "scared" money flies away quickly. Don't play that way. To win, you must play aggressively and with a sufficient bankroll to justify your level of action. All of this is covered in the other Keys to Winning. Discipline is the glue that holds it all together. Once the glue stops holding, it all falls apart.

WIN GOAL

What is a win goal? In simplest terms, a win goal is the realistic expectation of a certain win amount, based on the potential of available wins relative to the bankroll allowed, session stake allocated, expertise at the game, plus time at the game. This simple formula will equal your end-result profitability in winning situations, and your end-result saving of money that would have been lost in negative situations.

For example, most gamblers will say that a 2 percent win goal over and above the session stake is a very great achievement. The casino, for example, has a win goal of around 2 percent for most blackjack games, around an average of 4 percent for slots, and about 20 percent over all the games they offer. Some games will make them more money because people will play them badly. Although basic blackjack, for example, can be played to less than 0.5 percent casino advantage, most players will play the game so badly that the casinos actually yield anywhere from 2 percent to 6 percent, and often even more, on a game which can actually yield a *player* advantage if played properly and with skill (for more information on blackjack, I refer you to my book, *Powerful Profits from Blackjack*).

For slots, the average expectation is around 4 percent to perhaps 8 percent, depending on the casino, where it is located, and what the competition is like. In Las Vegas, the casinos mostly count on around 5 percent as their *average* win goal for all of their slots combined. Sometimes more, sometimes less, but overall around this figure. The reality, however, is that the slots will pay the casino much more. Overall, the casinos will get about 80 percent of their revenue from slots, and their average win-goal expectation over all their machines turns out to be around 12 percent, and sometimes more. The reason is primarily that slot players play so badly. They choose machines which don't offer the best value, or which offer low payoffs and low payback programs, and they generally play like blind hogs looking for an acorn.

The difference between the casino and the player is that the casino can easily have a much lower win goal because their doors are open 24/7/365. Their games make money all the time. Every hour, every day, every week, every month, every year, without ever needing a rest or a break. Human players can't play like that. While the casino can easily offer a game where it can reasonably expect less than 1 percent profit, it will get this all the time, always, over the short term as well as the long haul. You, the player, can't play like that. Therefore, whenever gamblers say to me that they expect a 2 percent return and consider this good, I politely tell them that's great, and quietly chuckle. These "gamblers" are trying to play like the casino, trying to beat the casino at their own game of survival. Trying to "outlast" the overall game percentages. This will result in nothing more than the gambler's eventual ruin.

Gamblers in general, and slot players in particular, must have win goals not only commensurate with their bankroll, session stakes, and so on, as listed earlier, but also with the realization that their exposure to the game will only be a very short slice of the game's overall event reality. Therefore, such win goals cannot and should not be measured in percentages relative to the way the casinos figure their own odds and win goals. Rather, these win goals should be measured in terms of what the game *can yield*, especially if played correctly, and if selected in accordance with the various selection criteria I listed earlier. It is also important at this point to introduce a derivative of the win-goal criterion, called the win expectation.

The win goal is what you have set as your desired objective, realistically based on the various principles already amply demonstrated. The win *expectation*, however, is based within the reality of the game itself and, most specifically, in that very short-term slice of that one specific game's event experience.

For example, if you are playing a $1 reel slot machine that takes 2 coins as maximum, with a session bankroll of $100, and whose top jackpot is $2,500, with a secondary jackpot of $800, your win *goal* should be the top jackpot and/or the secondary jackpot. Otherwise, why play it? However, based on the event occurrence of that specific very short-term slice of your exposure to this machine and game, your win *expectation* should be 20 coins. In this case, this comes to $20. This is a 20 percent improvement over and above your starting session stake. Where else can you get such a big return on your investment that quickly? And what if you don't hit the jackpots, and only make a $5 profit, falling far short of the win expectation as well as the win goal? Have you lost anything? You still made money. And that's the most important part of both your win goals and your win expectations. *Be glad you got what you got.* Remember, you are playing a slot machine, which means you are playing a game with a built-in house edge, and therefore *a game with a negative expectation.* This means the game will always make money for the casino in the end. If you hit it for *any* kind of a win, then you have caught the game at the right time and made money in spite of the fact that it's a negative-expectation game. If your stock rose by $5 per share, you'd be ecstatic, right? Well, why complain if your session at this slot machine only resulted in a $5 win? Any win means you have beaten the game. Be glad you did. Put it away, and set yourself up for the next session.

What if you lost, instead of winning? What if this machine was just a real dog, and no matter how well you selected it and played it, you just picked a bad one at a bad time? It will happen. In fact, overall, you will pick a winning machine, or have a winning session, only about 40 percent of the time. However, if you do it correctly, your overall wins will more than compensate for your losing sessions, and you will still wind up a winner. So this machine was a bad one, and your end-of-session result was a loss of $75. More than two-thirds of your session stake. This is about as bad as it can get. You suffered a 75 percent loss of your session bankroll—but the point is, you still have $25, or 25 percent, of your session stake left. It all adds up. Put it away, mark it as your session result, and move on to the next session. In the next session, you may have a $75 win. So with the sessions combined, you are even, and have accumulated slot club points and comps besides. What about the next session? There you may make $5. So now you are ahead by 5 percent, along with the accumulation of all your slot club points, comps, and freebies, and have done so in spite of the fact that your first session was such a devastating loss.

The point is that throughout your casino visit no slot playing session is ever independent of your other sessions. All your slot playing sessions are combined together to reveal, in the end as you go home, the entire block of all sessions combined. Whatever results you have achieved at that point determine your average per-session win-expectation percentage, and your win-goal achievement levels. You can use this information to more accurately reflect how well you played, and to modify your goals and expectations for future visits. But you must take *everything* into account, even the value of all the additions you have earned, such as your comps and freebies, and club points. All of this combines to affect your goals, expectations, and final relative results.

This now brings us to the final item in this chapter, and that is the overall win goal and overall win expectation. This is set by you based on bankroll, skill, and other abilities, as well as whatever other information and skills you may have acquired. If you have understood what I have attempted to illustrate, then your total win goal for your casino visit should be directly relative to your bankroll and comfort level at the games, as well as your other gaming and playing skills, including selection skills.

As a guide, your overall win *goal* should be to double your bankroll. Your win *expectation* should be to come home with 20 percent over and above your bring-in bankroll. If you achieve anything close to this, you have beaten the slot machines, and you have done what fewer than 1 percent of all casino players are able to do. You have become a good, knowledgeable, and responsible slot player. Congratulations!

Part Four

TALL TALES, TIPS, AND SECRETS

Odds and Ends

At this point, you may well ask, "Why is this chapter stuck right here in the middle of everything?" Because, dear friend, now is the time for three things. First, a little comic relief, by way of some stories and tall tales—each with slot hints, of course. Second, because there has to be a place where we can talk a little about some various aspects of slot play which don't fit in the other parts of this book, as well as some games which are odd, but which can be a very good, and profitable, part of your slot playing selection portfolio. Third, because there are many hints and suggestions which I would like to share with you.

I also want to discuss some of the most common questions, situations, and advice which I have been asked about over the past couple of decades, as well as things I have learned. All of this, of course, has a direct bearing on your proficiency as a profitable slot player. Each of the gems that follow includes something you should either have already learned, or will prepare you for some more good items which will be revealed a little later on, in Part Five. It all comes together in the end, and everything is essential for that total, cumulative, all-inclusive understanding. That's how you will get to the point of being able to make powerful profits from slots. So even if it is entertaining, it still has informative content, and meaning. It's fun, too.

WHICH ARE THE BEST SLOTS?

I am often asked this question. The answer used to be relatively simple. There were basically only two kinds of slots: the reel spinners with three to five reels as a standard, and the video poker machines. So the answer was that among the reel spinners, the three-reel machines with double-up symbols that also substitute for all the other symbols are the best to play. These mostly hold no more than 2 percent for the house, making the payback 98 percent (dollar machines and higher). Among the video poker machines, the best to play were the jacks-or-better 9/6 machines, or the 9/5 full-pay deuces wild.

Now, however, there are so many new machines that the answer is no longer simple. There are video slots with nine to twenty paylines (or more). There are numerous varieties of video poker games, all with different pay schedules and programs. So in order to answer the seemingly simple question of "Which slots are the best?" we now have to qualify that by dividing the machines into categories. Are we speaking about reel spinners? If so, are we discussing bonus games or progressives such as *Megabucks*® and *Wheel of Fortune*®? Are we speaking about $1 machines, $5 machines, quarters, or nickels? All these make a big difference in how you approach your play and how much you can expect to spend, and win.

Then there are the video machines. Are we discussing nine-line 45-coin-max nickels? Quarters? Are we speaking about 90-coin-maximum machines? Each is different, and each has widely varying features and pay programs. Then there's video poker, and for right now I don't even wish to get into that (my book *Powerful Profits from Video Poker* will be published soon). There aren't any simple answers to simple questions anymore.

So which *reel* slots *are* the best bet?

I made this point earlier in this book, but it bears repeating: The best kinds of machines to play are the three-reel, 2-coin-maximum with *double-up* symbols. Yes, *double symbols*. These double-up machines were some of the earliest derivative versions of popular reel slots, and they are still by far the best-paying machines in any casino. Look for the *Double Dollars*™ or *Double Diamonds*™ series of machines from IGT. The best ones can be identified by looking at the payoff display screen, to see if the key symbols say "double" on them. Of course, you need to be aware that all slot machines run in cycles, and therefore even these machines won't pay all the time. But they will pay more often than other kinds, and that's why I call them the best. By getting more pays for lesser betting requirements, you will last longer and give yourself not just more fun, but better chances for big wins.

Which are the best video slots?

Among all the machines now available, my personal favorites are *Double Bucks*™ by IGT, *Texas Tea*™, and the other games I listed in Part Two. These pay the best among all the new machines that I have played.

Which are the best progressives?

By far your best shot at winning something major is the $1 two-coin-maximum *Wheel of Fortune*® progressive. Think about it: It costs you only $1.25 more than the quarter version, but you get so much more for your wins. On the quarter game, when you hit the wheel for the 1,000-coin payout, all you get is $250, but on the $1 machine (where it costs you only $2 per spin), when you hit this same pay you get $1,000. And when you hit the jackpot, on the quarters you may get $800,000 or so, while on the dollar game you hit for over $4 million, on average. It's worth the extra buck and a quarter per pull.

What is the best slot play strategy?

There are several factors which can make your chances of winning better. *Selection* of the kind of machine to play is probably the most important. The *maximum-coin* requirement is another; so is *coin denomination*, which is directly relative to the size of your bankroll. *Not being distracted* by *in-casino promotions* is another, and so is *not being fooled* by the *nice-looking pictures* or *new-looking* machines, or great-sounding *high bonus jackpots*. The bigger the payoff, and the more large-pay combinations displayed, the harder it is to get them, and the more it will cost you. Also, don't play with the crowds. Traditionally, casinos are busiest on weekends, and particularly around dinner time—from about 5:00 P.M. to about 11:00 P.M. Your best choice is to wait until after all these crowds have pumped the machines full of money. Then you can come in when they all go home or go to bed. You not only have a bigger and better choice of available machines, but you're far more likely to strike a machine which has had a lot of play but hasn't paid out. So now *you're* the one who'll get the jackpots, while the herd from the night before has filled the slots full—just for you.

VIDEO KENO—THE MISUNDERSTOOD GAME

For many years the game of video keno has been misunderstood by most players. At the beginning, it just looked too complicated for players familiar with the simplicity of reel slots, or video poker. Video keno, however, is actually among the simplest slot machines to play. Yes, it is classified as a slot machine, since it is coin-operated and the playing principles are the same as in any other slot machine. As in Big Board Keno, the video keno game uses a screen with 80 numbers. After inserting a coin (or any number of coins, depending on what the maximum coins allowed for that game happens to be), you are then prompted by the machine to select your numbers. You can select from 1 to 10 numbers total on most regular video keno machines. In Big Board Keno, many casinos offer selections of 12 or more numbers, up to 20 total, and even more numbers when you play a "way" ticket. However, on regular video keno machines you can only pick up to 10 numbers total (some newer machines have "way" ticket type options, which I'll discuss a little later).

After you have selected the numbers you wish to play, the rest is simple. You press the "play" button and the machine plays the game. Whether you win or not depends on how many of your selected numbers are also drawn by the machine during that one game—just as in the Big Board Keno game played in the Keno Lounge. Payoffs vary, depending on how many numbers you selected, how many coins you played for that game, and how many of your selected numbers are hit. Don't worry about calculating what these payoffs are; the machine will automatically display the potential win amounts on the screen, either above the 80-number grid screen or to one side. Video keno is actually a very good game to play. Many of the payoffs for "straight-up" tickets—with marked numbers from 1 to 10—mirror the payoffs found in live keno, and often the payoffs on the machine are, in fact, considerably better than the Big Board Keno game. For example, the popular "6-spot" ticket normally pays off as follows (quarters):

		1 COIN	2 COINS	3 COINS	4 COINS
6 hits	=	$400.00	$800.00	$1,200.00	$1,600.00
5 hits	=	$17.50	$35.00	$52.50	$70.00
4 hits	=	$1.00	$2.00	$3.00	$4.00
3 hits	=	$0.75	$1.50	$2.25	$3.00
2 hits	=	$0.00	$0.00	$0.00	$0.00
1 hit	=	$0.00	$0.00	$0.00	$0.00
0 hits	=	$0.00	$0.00	$0.00	$0.00

As you can see, on this video keno ticket you have 4 chances out of 7 total to win. Also notice that if you play four quarters ($1) the payoff for a 6-out-of-6 hit (the top jackpot on this ticket) is $1,600 (*dollars!*), while most live keno games pay only $1,450 for this same $1 bet. Yes, there are several live keno games in many casinos where the payoffs on this 6-spot ticket are higher—some at $2,000 for a 6-hit for a $1 bet or even more—but these aren't as common as may be expected. Consequently, a 6-spot ticket on video keno is a good bet indeed. The same goes for many of the other number combinations you can select on a regular video keno machine. For many players, the problem regarding video keno has been that it just looks so complicated. That is a misunderstanding, since this game is about as simple as a casino game can get. Put your coins in, erase the previous card, select your numbers, and push "play." That's it. That's all you have to do to play video keno on all regular video keno machines.

There is another issue which needs to be addressed: video keno can be a slow game. Admittedly, not nearly as slow as the live keno game, where it may take anywhere from five minutes to thirty minutes to play just one game (depending on how busy the casino is and on the various policies for the game at the casino in which you happen to be). Video keno plays each game in about three seconds, and that is a distinct advantage for the players, because success in winning at video keno—as in keno generally—depends on the number of total games played. Frequency is your friend, as is speed of the game. Nevertheless, in order for you to be able to maximize the win potential on any ticket you play on a video keno game, you need to have patience, time, and bankroll. If you intend to play $1 at a time (four quarters on most video keno machines), you should have at least $200 as your available bankroll for that session. This should give you considerable play (since you have a total of 200 events at $1 per event with which to start) and will allow you to have the best possible chance at some significant wins along the way, even if you don't hit the major jackpot. Several of the advantages of video keno are that even secondary and tertiary jackpot hits amount to quite a sum of money. You can easily extend your playing sessions by recirculating these wins and continuing to play. I would advise you, however, that if you play more than 6 numbers, be ready to settle for the secondary jackpot. On a 7-spot ticket, for example, a $1 bet for a hit of 6-out-of-7 pays $400, and this is a good win indeed. For an 8-spot, the $1 bet for a hit of 7-out-of-8 pays $1,600 in most casinos; on a 9-spot ticket a bet of $1 pays $4,500 for a hit of 8-out-of-9, and on a 10-spot ticket a hit of 8-out-of-10 pays $1,000 for a $1 bet and $4,700 for a hit of 9-out-of-10 (in most casinos). These are all secondary jackpots (and a tertiary jackpot for the 8-hit on the 10-spot), and all are quite good pays for a small investment.

Another advantage to the video keno player is that the game can be played for as little as 25¢ per game. This means that all the payoff amounts I listed above will be paid at only one-fourth of the dollar-bet value, but it also means that your bankroll can be smaller. And even one-fourth of the above listed payoffs translates into significant wins, even if you play only 25¢ per game. I should warn you, however, that playing video keno can get tiring, and perhaps even boring. It requires patience, time, and dedication. Don't look to this game to give you an immediate winner (if you get one, you're very lucky indeed!). Most of the time this game requires that you invest time, as well as a sufficient bankroll. Don't be afraid to play the game for several hours. It is a good game and it does pay—with patience, persistence, and available bankroll. The best advice I can give you is:

Select your numbers and stick to them!

Frequently changing your numbers is video keno suicide. Pick your numbers in bunched groups, and then stick to them.

Frequency is your friend!

The longer you play, the more games you play, the greater your chances of hitting a significant winner. The machine is a computer, and the game is a numbers game.

Selections are picked at random by the machine after 1 coin is deposited, or 1 credit played, just like all the other slots. The longer you play on the same numbers, the greater your probability that the machine will, eventually, select precisely your combination of numbers. Don't be disappointed if your machine is not hitting anything in the first few pulls. That's the biggest mistake most players make, and that's why many people stay away from this game: they expect wins immediately, and in video keno such immediate hits are extremely rare. However, if you persist, and invest the time and bankroll, the more your machine is *not* hitting your number selections, the *better your probability* is for getting a very good winner.

With the ever-changing landscape of slot machines, the video keno machine has been the relative constant in casino electronic gaming. I play video keno almost exclusively for that very reason. By remaining virtually unchanged, video keno has stayed unaltered, and hence the possibilities of learning the various quirks and flaws in the game over the years have allowed me some considerable wins. But that kind of dedication is virtually out of reach for the average vacationing player, so the hints I am offering here are designed to give you the best chance at winning something in a relatively short term. So far I have won several jackpots of $3,550 and $3,335 on video keno, plus hits of $7,500 and $5,000, as well as numerous jackpots of $400, $750, and $1,175. All on video keno, and all because I practiced the principles I listed earlier: patience, and more patience, right number selections which I stick to, and not changing them per session, time and more patience. Sometimes it can take eight hours, or more, of constant play, but the wins are worth it. How many people can get paid $400 for an eight-hour day? Or $1,175 for eight hours? Or $3,550 for eight hours of work? Plus, *it is fun*!

NEW VIDEO KENO GAMES

In recent times, as computer technology allows, there have been several new variations on video keno available—primarily in Nevada, but increasingly so in most gaming jurisdictions. You may have already seen some of these machines, which may be multi-game machines such as the IGT Game King series. Such machines have video keno as one of their game options in the game menu. Playing these machines is just as simple as the older regular video keno machines, with the exception of the "touch-screen" technology, which allows you to use your finger to touch the screen to select your numbers instead of having to use a wand.

These new machines all employ the touch-screen technology, and on a special IGT machine in the Game King series, all versions of all the games are video keno games. Several of these games are actually similar to some of the "way" ticket options available in live keno. These video keno "way" ticket options allow players to play combination tickets, just as in the Live Big Board Keno game. Of course, the requirement is that you bet more to play these games, but the payoffs are often worth it since not only do you get more frequent payoffs, but also the payoffs multiply if your particular combinations are hit—again similar to what happens in the live keno games on such "way" tickets, when you "wheel" your numbers. On this IGT video "way" keno machine, the most commonly found game options are:

3-3-3: 9-Spot ABC "Way" Ticket

This is a game where you can select a combination of three 3-spots, for a total combination of 3/3, 3/6, and 1/9. You simply mark your ticket in three groups of 3 numbers. The first group of 3 numbers will be displayed on the machine as A-A-A, the second group of 3 numbers will be shown as B-B-B, and the last group of 3 numbers will be shown as C-C-C.

Hitting any 3-out-of-3 will pay you the amount of a single 3-spot win. Plus, if you also hit any of the other numbers, these combinations will make several pays for hits of 3s, 4-and-5-out-of-6, 6-and-7-and-8-out-of-9, and, of course, if you hit all three 3-spots, you not only get the three pays for the 3-out-of-3 hit, but you also get three 6-spot wins and one 9-spot win, plus all the smaller pays in between, all combined for one huge payoff.

The disadvantage of this version of video keno "way" ticket is the relatively expensive per-game cost: 7 coins to play all the above options, per game. This can get expensive, but you must also remember that this game will give you more frequent payoffs. Another, smaller disadvantage is that the game pays off at slightly lower payoffs, per combination hit, than would normally be found on the single straight-up single-card ticket. It's a trade-off, and you should keep this in mind.

Nevertheless, this is a good game to play, and the more frequent wins can more than compensate for the extra cost and the slightly lower jackpot totals. Of course, if you hit more than one of your selected combinations, these payoffs then multiply, and consequently you have made more money than you would make if you only played that one card on a single-card regular video keno game.

3-3 AB 6-Spot Ticket

This is a "way" ticket of two groups of 3 numbers, for a total of 2/3 and 1/6. It works on the same principles as all other "way" tickets, and similarly to the above description for the ABC combination ticket, except that here you only have the A-A-A and B-B-B ticket. The cost is 3 coins for maximum-coin play (advisable to activate all options, as is the case for all these video "way" ticket games).

4-4 AB 8-Spot Ticket

This is a version of an 8-spot ticket, where you are playing two 4-spots in combination: A-A-A-A and B-B-B-B. It works on the same principle I described above, except that here your combinations are 2/4 and 1/8.

King 9-Spot Ticket: 1/1 and 2/4 and 2/5 and 1/8 and 1/9

On this ticket you mark 1 King (meaning only 1 number, which is shown on the screen with a crown) and two 4-spots: A-A-A-A and B-B-B-B.

If you hit the King only, you will be paid even money for the 1-spot hit. If you hit any one 4-spot, you will be paid a reduced rate of one-fifth of the regular 4-spot payoff rate.

However, if you hit any 4-spot with the King, you will now be paid over $200, because you have not only hit the 4-spot, but also a 5-spot. Of course, if you hit more of the numbers, you get a multiplied payoff in very large sums. The cost is 4 coins for maximum-coin play.

5-6-7 ABC 7-Spot

This version allows you to play 1/5 and 1/6 and 1/7. The way this is marked is that the 5-spot will be shown as A-A-A-A-A, the 6-spot will be identified as B, and the 7-spot will be shown as C. In effect, you are playing for a 5-spot, a 6-spot, and a 7-spot. If you hit all the As, you get the 5-spot payoff. If you hit all the As with the B, you get the 5-spot plus the 6-spot payoff. And, if you hit all the As, with the B and the C, you not only get the 5-spot, plus the 6-spot, but now you also get the 7-spot for a huge win, plus all the little wins cumulatively in between. The cost is 3 coins for maximum play per game.

Top and Bottom

This is a popular ticket in the live keno games, and simply means that you are betting either that all the numbers will be at the top (or bottom) or that none of them will be at the top (or bottom). To play this version, you insert your coins—4 coins maximum—and then touch the screen for either all the Top-40 numbers or the Bottom-40 numbers. You win if a lot of the numbers show up, or if very few, or none, show up (whichever area you selected, be it top or bottom). In effect, you are playing both top and bottom, regardless of which area you select. If you get a lot of the numbers in your area (or all) you win big, and likewise if you get very few (or none) you also win big. For the payoffs, which are many and complex, I recommend you look at the payoff display available with the game. It will be clear once you look at it.

These "way" ticket video keno options are among the many which are fast becoming available for this game. One last reminder: Be patient. Video keno can be very profitable, but you must understand that it will take time on most occasions. So be prepared, sit down, and enjoy yourself.

Four Card Video Keno

I have recently become interested in a new multi-game machine by IGT in the Game King Series. What makes this machine different is that it is a *multi-denominational* touch-screen video slot machine with many different games. One of the features I like on these machines is the multi-denominational choices. These machines can be played for as low as one penny per credit, all the way up to $5 per credit. On the main menu screen are several buttons, each corresponding to the denomination of each credit wagered. For example, the first icon says "One Cent" and has the 1¢ denominational icon showing. Next to it is 2¢, then 5¢, then 10¢, then 25¢, then 50¢, then $1, and finally the $5 icon. This means that you can select the value of each of your credits. If you want to play any of these games in, say, nickels, you can touch the 5¢ icon, and this means that every game you choose thereafter will play as a nickel machine— and so on for all the other denominational choices available.

I like this arrangement because it allows you to progress your wagers. If, for example, you start playing the double-bonus video poker game with nickels, and the machine is hot, you can switch to the same game but in a higher denomination. You can go from nickels to, say, 50¢ per wager and thus maximize the machine's hot streak. Conversely, if your machine is starting to pay badly, you can either go to a lower amount per wager, or you can change games. Simply put, this kind of a machine offers you more choices, and if you take advantage of them you can do better with your game plan and win management.

One of the games I like most on these machines is a game called Four Card Keno. This video keno game has four cards, and you can play all four at the same time. You don't have to, but the whole point of this game is that you *can,* and because of this, you can quadruple your hits. Here's how it works:

First, you select the amount you wish to wager per credit. You do this by selecting the denomination icon of your choice on the main screen. Next, you touch the Four Card Keno icon, and this takes you to the game. Then, you choose how many credits you wish to play per card. You do this by touching the bet-one icon once for each credit per card. For example, say you want to play one credit per card. This means you will touch the bet-one credit button four times, and this will wager one credit for each of the four cards. Or you can touch the "bet max" button, and this will play the maximum wager per card, which is ten credits, for a total wager of forty credits per game. If you are playing the one-penny-per-credit, this means you will be wagering 10¢ per card, for a total bet of 40¢ per game. And so on for all the other denominations available.

Once you have selected the amount of the wager, you then touch Card A, and select your numbers. Then you go to Card B and repeat the process, then Card C, and finally Card D. Now you have selected numbers on all your cards. You then press the "deal" button, and the game draws the numbers. As in all keno games, the more numbers you hit, the more you win. But on this Four Card Keno game, the best advantage you have is that you can "wheel" your numbers. Wheeling numbers has been possible in lotteries for as long as they have been available, but until now it was not possible on video keno games. Wheeling your numbers simply means that you can select the same numbers on more than one card, so that when they hit you will be paid more than once for that hit. It is therefore a very good idea to pick a few core numbers, and then use these same numbers on multiple cards, along with whatever number extensions you choose.

For example: Say you wish to play a 6-spot as your main number selection. Pick your six numbers on Card A. Then, on Card B, pick the same six numbers, but add one more, for a 7-spot. On Card C, you can add, say, two more numbers for a 9-spot, and on Card D you can add one more number for a 10-spot. So now you are playing one 6-spot, one 7-spot, one 9-spot, and one 10-spot on all the four cards, with the original six-spot combination being common to all four cards. If you hit any of those original six numbers, these also count on all the other cards, thereby multiplying your wins.

Once you try this you will get the hang of it very quickly. You can experiment by yourself, and you will find that picking 9- and 10-spot combinations is usually the best, with at least six numbers of each group being common to the others. The bad news is that the payoff program on some of these machines is not nearly as liberal as on regular slots or video keno games, so you will need to keep in mind that you are facing a very large house edge on these games. However, on the Four Card Keno game this can be somewhat offset by the fact that you can get paid several times for a hit. It's fun, and I've had some nice hits on this game.

OTHER VIDEO SLOTS

Like it or not, we are now in the twenty-first century. What many of us have thought of as "futuristic" in years past, now seems all too common. The pace of change continues at seemingly breakneck speed. Innovations in slot technology, and the newest crops of slot machines, are just one testimonial to the fast-changing landscape of the casino floor. Already there are many video slot machines with multiple lines, and multi-coin play options. Some are cashless, and others multi-denominational. Popular themes abound, from history to pop culture to sports—the choices now seem endless. Most of these new slots are video slots, which offer a much greater variety of bonuses, second-screen features, and multi-line multi-coin play. I think it's a safe prediction that within the next ten years, perhaps even only five years, all slot machines on the casino floor will be video slots. Many will be available with three-dimensional images, perhaps even holographic slots. All of them will be cashless (or coin-free) machines, with multi-denominational features, multiple game choices, and in ever-increasing multi-line and multi-bonus versions. Many such video machines are already a staple of today's casinos.

To some traditional slot enthusiasts, these new machines may seem too complex and "gimmicky." While it is true that not all of these new machines are a better bet than the traditional reel spinners, the fact remains that the more machines there are, the better the choices for players. It is increasingly important to keep abreast of changes in slot machines and slot machine technology and to be able to select the *better* of the many varieties of choices which will continue to become available. Knowing your machine—and something more about it, such as its pay program and frequency of hits, value of bonuses, play and pay features, bankroll requirements for optimum play, and the many other factors which I have discussed in this book—will weigh even more heavily as the varieties of slot machines increase. Many slot players still shy away from video slots, thinking that they are too confusing: so many lines, so many symbols, so many pay combinations, bonus screens, bonus rounds, and so on. No need to worry. A video slot machine still works on the same principle as any other "reel" type slot machine. Spin the reels, line up the winning combinations, and you win that amount. Video slots only *look* confusing, largely because of the variety of various pay symbols and winning combinations. There are a few simple principles you should learn to enhance your video slot playing experience and your wins.

First and foremost, you should *always* read the "help" menu on the machine and learn the pay symbols: which symbol does what, which is "wild," which are "scatters," which substitute for which others, and so on. This will tell you what you need to hit in order to get the valued pay.

Second, learn how many coins are required to achieve the maximum win potential. Not all machines will pay the same for minimum-coin play, as opposed to maximum-coin play. Some will pay the second, third, and fourth bonuses only if maximum coins are played. Increase your fun and winning potential by increasing your knowledge of the game you are going to play. It's not hard, because all this information is usually available either on the machine's outside façade or, more likely, in the information which is stored within the machine (accessible by touching either the "help" icon or the "information" icon on the screen). In addition to this, here are some other key items to look for when choosing a video slot machine:

1. Look for machines which pay left to right *and* right to left. Many of the video slots only pay left to right—not as good a bet as those machines which allow pays to happen from both directions.
2. Look for machines which pay the winning combinations *cumulatively*. Normally, many machines will pay "only the highest winner," which means that if you get more than one winning combination you'll only be paid for the highest win. Since video slots are mostly multi-line machines, meaning there is more

than one active payline, it is better for you to play machines which will add up all the wins together, regardless of on which payline they were hit (most video slots will "pay the highest winner on *each active payline*," and this means they will pay the highest win, but pay this *on each played line* where any such win occurs, and, therefore, these pays will be added up). This is yet another reason why you should always play all lines, and with maximum coins bet.

3. Look for machines which have 9 or more paylines, and which also include the features from items 1 and 2 above. The more paylines you can play, the better your chances for a nice win.

4. Play maximum coins at all times. Many of these video slots allow you to bet up to 90 coins per bet, or even more in some cases. This may be a lot of money, but the pays are worth it when you hit any kind of winning combination. If you can't afford this many coins per bet, then at the very least you must play one coin *per payline*. However, you should not play any of these machines if you can't afford the maximum coins. Save up, and come back when you can afford it. It will make you a happier person, because now you will be getting the best the machine can offer.

5. Play 25¢ video slots rather than nickels. Nickel machines will cost you more to play than you can win, on some occasions (other than perhaps the top award or in case of a giant jackpot progressive). You will gain a better reward from quarter machines on just about every kind of *video* slot machine. Reel slots are different. The $1 and $5 reel slot machines are best. Also, some of the *newest* video reel slots, which may be in the base nickel denomination, are a very good bet, especially when you wager maximum coins on all lines.

6. Look for machines with multiple pay symbols which

substitute for the majority of other symbols, and also have "scatter" pays, all of which pay cumulatively. This will give you the best playing options, along with the kinds of features and playing principles described above.

These few hints will make your video slot play more enjoyable and also more profitable, and they can be applied to the vast majority of the new machines you will find in your favorite casino. The main catalyst for the growing variety of video slots is the improving computer technology which makes these games—and their many varieties and pay options—possible. What most people do not know is that almost all slot machines are now computerized, regardless of whether they appear to have mechanical-looking reels or whether they are just video displays on a video slot machine. It really doesn't matter these days, since the machines are practically all based on the same kind of computer platform. Yes, there are differences in slot machines from manufacturer to manufacturer, but as far as the slot players are concerned, modern slots are virtually all cloned from the same basic computer model. This may sound off-putting to some players—perhaps slot players used to more of the traditional-style slot machines—but these advances in computer technology are a *good* thing for slot players in general (and the casinos too, of course).

Casinos benefit from many factors, such as increased player interest, higher coins played per machine, and so on, but players also benefit, by having increased choices among machines to play, and even within the machines themselves. Many of the newest video slots are offered on the casino floor as multi-game machines, such as the IGT Game King™ series of machines and games. This simply means that there are several different kinds of games available on the one machine. This makes it easier for players to choose different games to play, offers increased entertainment and, in the end, also offers the kind of variety which is useful in increasing your wins. Probably the biggest benefit to the players is the fact that many of these new video slots offer choices in how much to bet. Some machines allow for play from 1 coin up to 90 coins per bet, or more in some cases. This means that the payoffs are also increased proportionally, allowing slot players to achieve higher wins per hit than was possible on the older-style machines. Another beneficial aspect of the newer video slots is the ability to choose the game speed. Some players prefer a slower pace to their game, while others prefer the game to play fast. I know I do. I find it infuriating if the games play slowly and I don't have the option to change the speed. However, on many of the newer video slots there's a screen icon which can be touched to select the speed of the game. This is a terrific innovation, because it lets you select how *you* wish to play, instead of having some programmer decide for you at what speed the game will play.

Just about every day there are new slots on the gaming floor. Casino executives feel that they must turn their machines over about every three months, otherwise the slot players will get bored with them. This is the short-attention-span fallacy. The casino executives who manage the slot floors are exposed to these games on a daily basis. Therefore, they assume that all slot players are likewise exposed, and therefore these slot players will get bored by having the same machines all the time. Wrong. In most casinos, players come and go, and new players come in and out all the time. Particularly in tourist destinations. So why keep replacing all the slots all the time? There are several reasons.

First, the slots have to perform to a specific income level. Many casinos no longer buy their slots, but rather lease the space the slot machine occupies on their casino floor in return for a cut of the slot drop (the money the machine makes from losing players). This is called "participation" and these slot machines are, therefore, called "participation slots." Not so long ago no casino would ever think of allowing "participation slots" on their casino floor. However, as computer technology evolves, and as newer machines are introduced by more and more manufacturers, casinos find themselves needing to turn their machines over to accommodate new ones. If they buy them, this can get expensive. At somewhere around $10,000 per machine, to buy 100 new machines which may last only four weeks, maybe three months, on the casino floor becomes a very significant expense, and one which the casinos can no longer easily recoup from the performance of the machines alone. Therefore, participating in the machine's drop, as opposed to having to buy it, makes more sense. Some casinos also lease the slots from the manufacturer for a daily fee.

Second, there are so many new machines coming out all the time. The casino floor has only so many spaces for slot machines. Even though there are now more casinos than ever before in the history of the United States, the fact remains that space is limited and the cost per machine and per casino floor space is rising. So casinos are always searching for those machines which are an instant hit with slot players, in order to make the most money from them as fast as possible before having to replace them.

Often machines get replaced too quickly, and for the wrong reasons. Just because a machine has been on the casino floor for three months doesn't mean that players are bored with it. If the machine's revenue drops, it may be for reasons other than lack of appeal to players. It has been my experience that machines tend to make less money for the casino when the casino starts firing the on-the-floor staff, such as change people, floor people, and drink servers. This results in lousy service, and therefore the machines appear to be performing less well. This, however, doesn't mean that the *machine* needs to be replaced.

Often players are lucky enough to find these new machines which play and pay quite well. There are many casinos where such machines can be found, especially if you learn to look for the good ones, like the IGT machines and games I mentioned earlier. Sadly, many casinos change these machines much too quickly, and too often. Instead of changing them, they should add more of their type, and concentrate on serving the needs of their customers, instead of on the erroneous perceptions of player-interest attrition. Lately it seems as if the slot players are being used more like research guinea pigs than casino customers. I don't like going to my favorite casino only to find that the machines I played yesterday are gone, having been replaced by the new crop of gimmicks which I know are short-lived, and will eat my money.

So what does all this mean for you? Don't be silent. Tell your favorite casino what your favorite machines are, and why. Help them out with their marketing studies. This will not only help your casino staff to give you better service, but will allow them to select and keep the kinds of slot machines you enjoy playing. That will be a true bonus for all of us who love to play the slots.

To help you select more of my favorite IGT slot machines, I have also decided to mention some of the more established machines and games which I have personally played. These are in addition to the ones I listed earlier, and are games which have most likely already been in your favorite casino for several months. I again remind you that video slots are different from *reel* slot machines. While I advise against playing quarter and nickel games in the reel-style machines, the video slots are directly the opposite. Particularly for quarters, which are the better bet among video slots. However, the nickel-based games are also very good, especially if you can bet 45 coins, or more, as maximum coins. This will often give you better payback percentages than even the good traditional reel spinners.

Black Rhino™

This is a five-reel video slot machine game with nine paylines. The extensive pay table, which features wild animals and African flowers, offers a range of unique payouts. A "Dancing Masks" feature is also added, where these masks pay when hit in any scattered position within the viewing screen. The "black rhino" symbols also substitute for all Ace, King, Queen, Jack, 10, and 9 symbols, offering even greater variety of pays. In addition, on most of these machines players can also choose to play up to 45 coins per game. This is a good game to play. Its one disadvantage is that it pays only from left to right, except for the "Dancing Masks" which pay when two or more of them are hit anywhere in the pay window regardless of on which payline they are.

Diamond Mine™

This is a five-reel five-line machine with a second-screen bonus feature. When "sparkle" symbols line up on the payline, the machine automatically activates the second-screen bonus feature. Once activated, the player is then prompted to help the miner pick a barrel to blast the mine and find the bonus prize. Unlike *Black Rhino*™, this game pays both left to right and right to left, making it a slightly better bet. The disadvantage is that this is only a five-line game and does not generally have the option of betting more than 25 coins per game.

Super 8 Race™

This is an eight-line race-car-themed game that features special pays for like symbols in the corners, an all-fruit bonus, and a "turbo mode." When the "turbo mode" is activated—by hitting the race car symbols lined up in a "diamond" configuration—free plays are offered. In the subsequent series of such free plays, each time a race car symbol appears on a payline (and only in this turbo mode), the player is paid ten times the bet. This game pays left to right, but there are eight reels so the payoffs are often multiplied.

Royal Riches™

This game combines the video-reel slot machine game with a video draw poker game. The game is a five-reel five-line video slot machine, with the added feature of "scattered coins." When these "scattered coins" appear correctly in the window, free draw-poker games are awarded. These poker games have a "fantasy" payoff. Check the pay chart on the machine for further details.

Double Bucks™

I love this game! A derivative of the *Black Rhino*™ machine, this game uses many of the same-style symbols. It has proven to be very popular in Australian casinos. This game is a five-reel nine-line video slot machine, with the added option of a maximum bet of up to 45 coins per game. Players can double the payoffs when matching a scale symbol to other paying symbols. If you hit three or more "scattered coin" symbols you'll get ten free plays. While in the ten-free-plays mode, all payoffs hit are *tripled*. There are numerous payoff possibilities on this game, and I therefore suggest you carefully read the pay chart and help menus. With these available pay options, this is also one of the better multi-line games to play. In fact, among all these games, this one is perhaps the most lucrative to play. I have personally hit these machines in excess of 10,000 credits on many occasions, and also have hit many of the top jackpots. This machine is among my favorites for all these reasons.

As with all of the slots I have described throughout this book, the Keys to Winning apply here as well.

WHERE TO PLAY

Finally, I wish to focus on *where* to play. This is a choice you must make in the selection of the casino in which you will make your slot playing investment. In the Midwest, there are many casinos whose slots offer some of the better payouts, and whose slot clubs offer many valuable incentives. Among some of the casinos I like are Kewadin Casinos (I like the Sault Ste. Marie and St. Ignace properties in Michigan), Soaring Eagle Casino at Mount Pleasant, Michigan, Fortune Bay Casino in Minnesota, Ho-Chunk and Oneida Casinos in Wisconsin, and the Meskwaki casino in Tama, Iowa. For those of you who may be planning a trip to the East Coast, Foxwoods and Mohegan are both excellent tribal gaming properties, with many of the best slots to be found in casinos anywhere.

Perhaps you are planning a trip to Nevada. If you are, I would like to recommend that you pay a visit to the Silver Legacy Hotel and Casino, or the Reno Hilton, or the Peppermill, all in Reno, Nevada. Reno in the winter is a picturesque city, with many winter activities nearby, and a host of casinos with good value for slot players.

Of course, there's no place like Las Vegas. If this is your destination of choice, then some of the best casinos for you to visit are Bellagio, Caesars Palace, Mirage, Bally's, Paris,

Monte Carlo, Mandalay Bay, the two Hiltons, Venetian, Aladdin, MGM Grand, Tropicana, Excalibur, Luxor, and the many others on the Strip and Downtown. All have a good selection of video slots, as well as most of the better-paying reel slots. For smaller casinos off the Strip, you may want to check out Arizona Charlie's West and East, the Palms, or the Station Casinos in any area. Also, remember that these casinos in Las Vegas get the hottest new games the fastest, so start planning your trip now.

Vegas Stories and Tall Tales

No book about slots would be complete without at least a few zany stories. All of these stories are true, either witnessed by me, told to me directly by the people involved, or told to me by people whom I trusted to "tell it true."

MYSTIC SLOTS

Got your attention? Are we going to delve into slots mysticism in this chapter? I know quite a few slot players who actually do this, in an effort to coax the magic jackpot out of the machines. I'm fond of telling two stories about two very nice people who had the most unusual way of playing slots.

One was an East Indian gentleman who used to come to the old Frontier hotel in Las Vegas, many, many years ago. He would find his favorite slot machine, place a wicker basket in front of it, pull out a flute, and begin to charm a real cobra! As the snake rose majestically out of the basket, swaying to the mystical sounds of the man's flute, he would play his machine. Unfortunately the other players weren't so fond of the snake, and so Security appropriated it and the gentleman was never seen again.

The other story is about a nice man who used to play the slots at Caesars Palace in Las Vegas. He was of oriental ancestry, a doctor, and an avid slot player. He would arrive with a whole slew of knickknacks, among which were a Buddhist shrine and several samurai swords. He would then select his machine and build an entire shrine around it, complete with crossed samurai swords. He dressed up in a wild outfit, complete with robe, swords, and daggers, and he would then play the machine. The staff at Caesars allowed him this privilege, not only because he was a very good customer, but also because his activities did not cause any other customers concern. This man would roam around Caesars resplendent in his robes, swords, and daggers and merrily play his machines.

Neither of the above two stories resulted in any "mystic" benefit, but they do point to the fact that many slot players wish they could invoke some mystical power to help them win the jackpot. For those of us who are mere mortals, however, there are several principles of slot play we can employ to assist us with our selection of game, machine, and play, as I have shown in this book.

THE SLOT WIZARD

Some time ago I had several friends with whom I played slots. This was in the long-ago past—in slot machine terms—which is now ancient history. At that time, most of the modern slot machines which can now be found in the casinos didn't even exist. Yes, there were the video poker machines and the reel slots, and they are both part of this story, but they weren't of the kinds now available. Video poker machines were mostly the basic jacks-or-better, some with the beginnings of bonus games, deuces wild and jokers wild, but that was about it. And the reel slots were the standard three- and four-reel types, with some video reel slots, but those weren't nearly as sophisticated, nor as popular, as the current crop of their kind is now.

My friend was at the time a host in one of the top casinos in Las Vegas. A good friend to have (who also had other friends in the business), since this allowed for good knowledge, not to mention the free-flowing comps. Boy, we lived well then! There were a number of very interesting characters who would visit this particular high-end casino in Las Vegas in those days. My friend and I, along with a few others, comprised at the time a kind of club. We would go out and play slots together, often as a team, and sometimes as a two-man team. There were many different kinds of video poker and slot machines then which we would know about, and know what kind of play they got and when they were about to hit. We would go from casino to casino and play them, and we had some very good hits.

For those of you who may not know this, in Las Vegas (and Nevada in general) slot machines, and video poker machines in particular, can be found in supermarkets, gas stations, convenience stores, and bars. This seemed odd to me when I first encountered it but one gets used to it eventually. A benefit of this was that many of these convenience stores and supermarkets had in-house progressives, mostly on the video poker. These video poker machines were often played extensively by shoppers, and mostly not with the maximum coins in, so the progressive jackpots for the royal flush would grow to quite large proportions. My friend and I would go out late at night, after he finished work at 2:00 A.M. or so, and we would go to the various convenience stores and supermarkets and play all the machines. Usually there were only three or four machines linked to the progressive, so at that hour we would each play two machines. This way we had all the machines covered. Eventually one of us would hit the jackpot, and then we would divide the money and go elsewhere.

Of course, there were times when we didn't win. One time we were playing a $1 progressive video poker machine whose jackpot was well over $6,800 at the time. We weren't doing well and were down to our last 25 coins. So my friend and I decided to try to build our bankroll by playing less than maximum coins, and played 2 and 3 coins instead. Well, what do you think happened? We were dealt a flush in diamonds: A-K-Q-J and a 9. We needed the 10 of diamonds. Discussion ensued. Should we keep the flush for the coins (which we needed badly at that time), or go for the royal? We had 3 coins played at that point. We went for it and got the royal flush. However, instead of being paid the $6,800 jackpot, we only got $750. We never forgot this, and from that point on we always played maximum coins.

This friend of mine was truly a slot wizard. He would also play the reel slots, and had a very good system, or principle of playing going for a while. He would find a bank of slot machines which were all 2-coin $1 slots, about five to six machines in a row, and he would then play *all* of them at the same time. He would play one, then move to the next, play that, then the next and so on, and when he reached the last one, he would repeat the procedure in reverse. Whenever he won some coins on one, he would cash them out and use that as ammunition for continued play. Many times we would rack up stacks and stacks of coin racks, over several thousand dollars. This was truly a sight to behold. There he was, pumping coins into all these machines at the same time, with coin trays full and racks stacked up the sides of the machines. Often I would come to help him play, and to assist him in the physical demands of playing all these machines at the same time and handling the heavy coins. It was a lot of fun. It didn't last, of course, since we weren't employing any kind of consistent system at that time, but I like to think back on those days when it all seemed easier, somehow.

ANOTHER WIZARD

The previous story and others like it, are part of the folklore of slot players. There is always a lot of interest in people who win and how they did it. That's one of the reasons casinos have a "Hall of Fame," usually an area of the casino where they frame photographs of slot winners, mostly the big winners. Yes, it is certainly very nice to win a large jackpot, but there are many slot players who win smaller jackpots, from $400 to $2,500 or so, and mostly they do not get to have their picture taken, posted on the "Hall of Fame" wall, or published in the casino's slot club magazine.

Many years ago I met a young man whose particular slot wizardry was quite interesting. I met him incidentally; a friend recommended that I contact him to repair the brakes on my car. Apparently he was moonlighting as a "fix-it" man, while also working as a casino porter in one of the mid-range casinos in Las Vegas. One wouldn't think that a person who does these kinds of jobs would have success as a slot player, but in all honesty it isn't appropriate, or useful, to make such judgments about people without getting to know them. I didn't give this any thought at the time, because my purpose was to have my car repaired, and not to talk slot play. As it turned out, we got to know each other during the process of having my brakes repaired. I was writing my first book at the time and we got to talking, and that's when he shared his story with me.

This fellow, let's call him Bob, hit upon the idea of combining a few elements together to arrive at a slot machine selection and playing principle. Gaming authors often advise our readers to first learn something about the casino games they are about to play and, in the case of slot machines, about the machines themselves, and their different kinds. Also, we usually advise players to do research. For slot machine play, such research can take the form of spending time in the casino during busy times and watching which machines get played, how they play, and how they pay. Then, after accumulating this kind of knowledge, return later, when the casino is not that busy, and divide your play among the various slots you observed earlier being played a lot and not paying out a lot. Although this technically does not assure you of a win, it is nonetheless one of a series of good methods to make your machine selections. Such information can be useful in helping you decide which machines should be better candidates for your gaming investment. Certainly, machines which get a lot of play are among those whose cycles are circulated more often than those machines which aren't played as much. The thought being, therefore, that for your play it is better to let others play the machines extensively and, provided that no significant payoffs happened during the time you studied this play on these machines, your investment can be, and indeed often is, more profitable, with more frequent pays and, likely, also some of the jackpots.

Well, as Bob would tell it, these factors were among his favorite selection criteria. He got himself a job as a casino porter so he could observe the slot play and also get paid for being around there. Of course, he had to do this in a casino which allowed its employees to gamble when off duty. Some casinos will allow that, while others won't, but generally, once the employee is off duty, where they go and which casino they patronize is up to them. Bob had quite a wide range of choices. He selected this mid-range casino in Las Vegas because it was one of those which got a lot of tourism traffic. He would work his shift, and while working, he observed which machines were getting a lot of play. Then, later—much later, in fact on graveyard—he would come back as a customer and begin to play the machines he had observed being played a lot during the previous day.

His method was quite simple. He would concentrate on particular carousels, which are banks of slot machines grouped together. During his research time, he would keep an eye out on two or three such carousels in the area of the casinos where he worked most often. Then, when he returned to play, he would know which of the carousel machines got the most play, and would begin by buying a rack of $1 coins. He always played $1 or $5 reel slot machines, never anything else. Once he bought his rack of coins, he would approach each of the machines he selected, in turn, and play one 20-coin stack in each machine. On these machines this meant either ten pulls for a 2-coin-maximum machine, or about six pulls for a 3-coin machine. He would always play maximum coins. This meant that he had five of these events available for each rack—there are five 20-coin grooves in a rack of coins ($100 for $1 coins and $500 for $5 coins).

As he would move along the carousel playing this way, he would concentrate on how each machine was playing. If among his ten or so pulls per machine he began to receive pays, he would stay with that machine and play. If he did not receive significant pays for that span of events, he would move on to the next machine in his selection and repeat the process. He would always stop playing if he either won a rack of coins, which meant $100 for a $1 or $500 for a $5 machine, or hit either the secondary or primary jackpot. But always only on his initial set of pulls, with continued play being from accumulated wins. His bankroll was always five racks of $1 coins ($500) or three racks of $5 coins ($1,500). Plus, if he had significant wins on the $1 machines, such as hitting a jackpot over $2,500, he would then do a session on the $5 slots, following the same principles. This seemed to work well for him.

By the time I met Bob, he had accumulated $75,000 in wins for that year. That was his goal, as he said. Soon after that, he left town. As far as I know, he opened an auto repair shop somewhere on the East Coast. I never saw him again.

Part Five

WINNING HINTS AND STRATEGIES

The Pseudo-RNG

Gaming literature, particularly books and articles on slot machines, is full of references to the RNG—the Random Number Generator. This is often described as the program which randomly selects the winning combinations, running constantly until it is triggered by the deposit of the first coin, or credit played. However, no one thus far has told us what it really is or how it works. In reality, there is no such thing as an RNG. What there is, is a computer program, *part* of which is what is usually described as a Binary Numerical Sequencing Algorithm. What this means is a series of sequenced numbers in binary code, which form the basis for an illusory program offering a sampling randomization. Since nothing can be programmed to be truly random, this method of acquiring random sequences produces the illusion of randomness, to a mathematical model and formula, which can be sufficiently quantified to produce the desired verifiable results, and thus allow for the slot machine to pass regulatory testing and compliance standards.

While I was researching material for this book, I wanted

to offer something more about slot machines than is normally found in books and articles on slots. I thought it would be interesting to find out what the RNG really is and how it works. Is there really such a thing? The conclusion I reached is this: There *is* a program that can be *called* an "RNG," which is part of another program, which is part of yet another program, and these programs, working together, are what allow the modern computerized slot machine to function in the manner in which it does. However, this program is really not a true RNG, as it is commonly understood. The moniker "RNG" is just an oversimplified way of expressing the reality. To understand what I mean, I offer you the following extract from a series of conversations I had with my friend Dan ("Dan" is not his real name.). The content of what follows is not all there is—just all that is possible to include in this book, to offer a glimpse into the real workings of the slot machine, for the purpose of letting you know exactly how, and why, it works, and works the way it does.

"Slot machines are controlled by programs, and these programs are stored on a computer chip, called an EPROM (Erasable Programmable Read Only Memory). The chip is in a sealed location on the printed wire board, and changing it, or taking it out, is not a trivial matter. A lot of paperwork has to be filled out, and there is quite a procedure to follow in order to take the slot off line, change out the chip (perhaps change the belly glass), and then put the slot back on line. The EPROM contains, among other things, the Virtual Reel Table. Though the player sees the Actual Reels— spinning behind the glass or simulated on a video display— these reels are *only a display* to show the player *what has already been determined several seconds earlier*. In a lot of cases, the Actual Reels will contain 11 symbols and 11 spaces, for a total of 22 positions. On a 3-reel machine, that means that there would be 22 to the third power—(22^3)—the number of possible combinations, in this case 10,648. If there was only one jackpot symbol on each reel, then *some* players might imagine that the odds of hitting all three jackpot symbols would be one in 10,648. They are dead wrong! Actually, the odds of hitting the jackpot, or *any* winning combination for that matter, are *not* determined by the Actual Reels, or the number of symbols and spaces on those reels.

"The real odds of hitting the winning combinations, are determined by the *Virtual Reel Table*. This information is *never* made available to the player.

"Every slot machine comes from the factory with a specific Virtual Reel Table and a specific Pay Table. The player can see the Pay Table, but they can never see the Virtual Reel Table. There is also another document that comes with every slot machine, and that's called a Par Sheet. This Par Sheet tells the casino the exact odds for every winning combination on the slot machine in question, and also tells them what the "long-term" Payout Percentage is for that particular machine. There are also some other pieces of information on the Par Sheet—one of those is the hit frequency. Hit frequency has to do with how often something will be paid back to the player.

"The Virtual Reel Table, in combination with the Pay Table, determines the actual "long-term" Payout Percentage for any given slot. The Virtual Reel Table is usually populated with many more symbols and blanks (ghosts) than what the player sees on the Actual Reels. For instance, it is not uncommon for the Virtual Reel Table to contain 63 or even 127 different virtual stops. For 63, that would allow 250,047 possible combinations and 127 would allow 2,048,383. Obviously, this makes it possible for machines with only 22 symbols on the Actual Reels to offer a Jackpot prize of much greater than only 10,000 coins.

"Now about the RNGs—it is tough to write a good RNG.

We all know that in actuality a better term would be *pseudo-*RNG, since anything that is programmed is not truly random. However, there are ways to make a pseudo-RNG look, to a slot player, like a true RNG. It is also a reasonable opinion that all RNG routines are written to produce a very basic random distribution of numbers. Once this is done, it is up to the Virtual Reel Table and the Pay Table to account for the actual Payout Percentage.

"G.L.I. (Gaming Labs International) is one of the largest slot machine testing agencies. When a slot machine is submitted to them for testing, the randomness of the output must pass a stringent chi-square test—and if it doesn't, the slot cannot be sold to the casinos. Here is basically how the slot programmers accomplish the task of creating a "perfect" distribution of numbers.

"Say we wanted to have a routine that would give us a "perfect" distribution of numbers from 0 to 9. To be completely random, and completely fair, we would want to see each number the same number of times. In other words, if we ran this generator 100 times, we would expect to see 10 zeros, 10 ones, 10 twos, etc., etc. Now, one way this could be accomplished would be to simply start with a "seed" of 0 and then add one to it each time. Of course the numbers would be coming out *in* order, rather than in a *random* order.

"Well, there is a software routine that is a well-known algorithm that will accomplish just exactly what we want done. It's called a Linear Feedback Shift Register (LFSR). It's a little complicated to explain here, but, basically, it is a register of bits, and each time a clock pulse clocks the register, a bit falls out one end of the register, and it is "exclusive-0-Red" with one of the middle bits, and is fed back into the start of the register. It's easier to see this routine in action than it is to try and explain it. If we had a 4-bit register, there would be 15 non-zero combinations that this register could produce. Obviously, an LFSR will not work with all zeros loaded into it for a seed. However, any one of the 15 possible non-zero combinations can be loaded into it, and then if clocked, it will produce exactly one instance of all the 15 possible combinations, and then start all over again. What's even nicer is that it will produce these combinations in a random order, rather than a sequential order.

"In a real slot machine, the LFSRs contain a lot more than just 4 bits. It is more than likely that they would contain 32 bits. With 32 bits, there are a *lot* of possible combinations. In fact, the total number of possible combinations is 2^{32}, or 4,294,967,296 total combinations. Say the LFSR is clocked at a rate of 1,000 times a second—again, not an unreasonable number. In this case, we can see that for the LFSR to generate *just one* full cycle of combinations, it would take 1,193 hours, or approximately 49 days. That's assuming the power is on 24 hours a day—if it is, the LFSR is running through combinations whether or not anyone is playing the slot. So, when a player puts in a coin, or pulls the handle, or presses the Spin Reels Button—it really doesn't matter what the trigger is—the program goes out to the LFSR and gets the next 3 bit patterns that happen to be being generated at that instant in time. Of course these 32 bit patterns equate to decimal numbers that are 0 to 4,294,967,296. If you recall, the Virtual Reel Table only contains 63 positions on each reel. Therefore, these raw numbers must be divided by 63, and then everything is thrown away except for the remainder. This process is known as modulo arithmetic, and will result in numbers from 0 to 62. The program then takes these three numbers and looks them up in the Virtual Reel Table, in order to determine which symbol on the Actual Reels to display. If it is a winning combination, it will cue the Credit Meter to credit the player with the appropriate number of coins.

"There is one other thing. Since 4,294,967,296 is being

divided by 63, that means that essentially *each* of the 63 positions is really mapped to 68,174,084 combinations from the LFSR, and since there are 1,000 numbers per second being generated, we actually can see the entire range of 63 numbers occur about 16 times a second. Therefore, we aren't waiting for 50 days to have the possibility of seeing the entire range of 63 numbers occur for any one of the reels. This is how I understand these things to work, and this is how it must be in order to pass the tests at G.L.I."

Now you know what a slot machine really is. In its reality, it has nothing to do with the pretty pictures you see on the reels. It has nothing to do with the number of stops on the actual reels you see, or the number of spaces on them. It all runs from the virtual reel table, in accordance with the programs as outlined above. It's simply and purely a matter of numbers. The results of the combinations are merely numbers themselves. The pictures you see on the reels are merely the graphics that are made possible by the graphic interface, on video reels, and by the command to display just that combination on the traditional-looking reel machines.

To be able to make a machine which holds as close as possible to these "randomness" standards, the manufacturer sends the Par Sheets to the testing labs. These Par Sheets contain, among other things, the following information:

1. Long-term payout percentage
2. Probability of each winning combination
3. Odds of each winning combination
4. Pay table
5. Win frequency
6. Hit rate
7. Date of manufacture
8. Serial number

By manipulating values, the payout can be adjusted up and down. This then allows for the availability of different payback percentages and therefore different pay tables and house "hold" on games which appear identical. That's why one casino can have the game set at a payback of, say, 98 percent, while another casino can have exactly the same game set at the payback of 94.7 percent. The adjusted sheet then reveals the contents of the virtual reel table for any given payout percentage. And that's the true story of the RNG for slots.

Questions and Answers

Since we are getting close to the strategy portions of this book, now is a good time to reflect a little on what we have learned so far, and perhaps add a little to it. In keeping with the simplification principle, the following are some simple questions offered along with—I hope—simple answers.

How do slot machines pay off?

Since nothing can be truly random, as we have just shown above, machines pay off in cycles. Although the general perception is of complete randomness, the truth is that the machines will select the bits in cyclical events. Sometimes these will allow the machine to pay more than its preprogrammed percentage, and at other times, it will pay less. In the end, at the final tally at the conclusion of each fiscal year life cycle of each machine, the percentages will roughly equal the preprogrammed payback percentage, or come as close to it as is statistically possible, and within the acceptable regulatory standards for such a range as defined in the approval process. Therefore, for you to win, you must catch the machine during times when it will hit the cycle of bits which translate to winning events. To do this, use the Keys to Winning, as well as the other information offered throughout this book.

How do they make money for the casino?

By "holding" that preprogrammed percentage, over all events, and over all the time the machine is powered. If the preprogrammed "hold" percentage is 2 percent, then the machine will hold at least that, depending on play. Some machines require the players to wager maximum coins in order for it to pay at the proper preprogrammed rate. Other machines require player skill, and therefore if they are played badly, will hold more. For this reason, even machines which may be programmed to "over 100 percent payback" can still hold money for the casino, and thus make a profit for the casino, because many players will play these machines either without the maximum-coin wager, or just play them badly. Good play, skillful and knowledgeable play, combined with always wagering the maximum coins, will equal profits from your slot play closest to the optimum payback percentage of each such machine. You will, therefore, force the machine to hold less for the casino.

How do we know which ones are the better payers, and which ones are the takers?

You can't. Not exactly, and not all the time. What *is* possible is *knowledgeable selection* of the machine and game—read again the Game Selection criteria in the Keys to Winning. However, there are some hints. Look for slot islands among reel slots. Look for simple pays and multipliers. Among video slots, look for games which can be easily understood, and which offer frequent bonus hits. Finally, look for IGT machines as a brand name. These are always among the best-paying machines in any casino.

Where are the best-paying machines?

For reel slots, look for slot islands in areas of the casino which can be seen from different vantage points. Walk around, and find the banks of slots which can be seen from just about everywhere in the casino, or as many points as possible. These are the most visible slots, and these will traditionally be set the loosest. For video slots, or other reel slots, look for areas which are about halfway between the pit and the other common areas of the casino. Stay away from machines which are near the table games pit, or near the showroom lines, buffet lines, coffee shop, gift shop, or any other area where there are other things to do. Also, many casinos put their best-paying machines in front of, or near, the main casino cage. This is so that those people cashing in, or cashing checks, will see people winning and will spend some of their money in these machines as they are leaving the cage. It's smart to look for this.

Where do the casinos put their good machines, and where do they put the bad ones?

See above. Also, sometimes the good machines can be found in hard-to-see areas, where few people go. This can be because the casino wants to attract players to that area. However, most of the time the above item serves to answer this question.

How can we tell the difference between different machines, if they look the same?

Look at the pays on the belly glass if it's a reel slot machine, or the "pay" screen if it's a video slot machine. Also, look at the top jackpot amounts, or even the top two or three jackpots, for maximum-coin play. The differences in these amounts will indicate which kind of machine this is, as compared to others which may look the same. Another hint is to look at the multiplier symbols, and bonus pays and bonus rounds. These may be slightly different, but sufficiently so for you to discover this if you look for it. For example, on the reel slots, one machine may have multiplier symbols which also substitute for all other symbols, while another machine that looks identical may have these same symbols, but they are only "wild," although otherwise they look the same. On video slots, some of the machines may have only five lines, while another one that looks exactly like it will have nine lines or more. Also, on some of these, the minimum pays may be limited to only some lines, with some "wild" symbols working only on the first and fifth (or last) reel, while on other machines that look the same, these can pay anywhere. Some of these may only pay left to right while others, which look the same, may pay from both sides. It's up to you to take the time to find this out.

How should we play the machines to our best advantage?

Always play maximum coins. If you can't afford this, don't play until you *can* afford it. Don't play without an adequate bankroll, which allows you to play with sufficient capital to wager maximum coins, and force the machine to pay back at its optimum preprogrammed percentage, and to pay you the maximum pays which are available. Don't play affected by alcohol, sleep deprivation, drugs, or any other chemical. Play rested, and play focused. Select the better machines, and play with enough of a session stake to give the machine the best play you can. Read "Keys to Winning" again.

What strategy, if any, can we use to get the most value from our slot machine dollars?

What I call the Simple Strategy for Slots, and the Big Secret follow below. None of this, however, will matter if you don't follow, at the very least, two key items of preparation and discipline. One: Play with a dedicated and sufficient bankroll, made up of money which is free and unencumbered and not "scared." Two: Play rested, emotionally stable, and without being affected by alcohol, drugs, or any other casino distraction.

What about the bill acceptors?

They make many games possible. Video slots could not be possible in the multi-line and multi-coin formats if we didn't have bill acceptors (also known as "currency acceptors"). They are an easy way to insert your money and play the machines. Unfortunately, many of them don't work very well, and are often broken and remain unrepaired by the casinos. Also, if your currency has any kind of markings, like those black lines which casino cage people put on the bills, then the currency acceptor will reject the bill. Sometimes even a minor imperfection will cause the bills to be rejected, even if this tiny imperfection was part of the minting process. For example, many bills are cut by the U.S. Mint with small borders on one side of the bill. The bill acceptors will reject these bills, because they read them as "altered" when, in fact, they are perfectly accurate and correct currency bills. These problems often cause player frustration, because sometimes you can keep sticking bill after bill after bill into these acceptors, and all of them will be rejected. However, as technology improves, this is also being overcome. Soon all bill acceptors will not only be able to accept various currency, but also be able to tell the difference between a counterfeit bill, and one which is authentic, but merely marked, or just has short borders, or some other small irregularity. This will help ease the player complaints, and the frequent jams which the current bill acceptors often experience.

What about the slot clubs?

Always join the slot club, if one is available at your casino, regardless of whether or not you plan to play slots. Most casinos will have a slot club, because it helps them keep track of their good players and other customers they otherwise may have missed. Even if you are not planning to play slots at that casino, you may become interested in playing some machines after you look around, and so joining the slot club will only help you. Most casinos will offer some kind of an incentive to join, such as a free buffet, a two-for-one dinner, a show, extra points, or something like that. Many Las Vegas casinos, from time to time, also offer a guaranteed "no loss" policy for new members of their slot club, usually up to $100. This means that if you don't book a win during your first playing session (24 to 48 hours, mostly), the casino will refund you up to $100 of your total loss. It's a nice way to enjoy the slots, and that casino, and to know that no matter what happens, you will get at least some money back.

Most of the time, joining the slot clubs will bring you benefits later on. If you play slots for even short amounts of time, your play will accumulate. The casino will then recognize you as one of their preferred customers, and you are likely to begin receiving lots and lots of special perks. Most often, you will receive an immediate invitation to return, and this may include free rooms, food, beverages, or at least discounted rooms and other offers, depending on your level of play. Some casinos also offer cash back for your earned points, and therefore it is always a good idea to join the slot club in every casino you visit. If you are a frequent casino visitor, and come to destinations such as Las Vegas, which has many casinos in a relatively small area, then you can easily join several slot clubs at once. Most of the time you will get at least something from each of them, and so you can easily get perks from several casinos, even if you don't play there, or don't play there very much. You may, in fact, find out that this casino is very good, and then be able to come back to it again and again. At the very least, you will be able to visit several different casinos and experience their slot clubs.

You should always compare the clubs, because they are all different, and sometimes *very* different. While at one casino, you may qualify for a free dinner after, say, 200 earned points, at another casino this may take 2,000 earned points. Always find out how many dollars through the machine—known as "action"—it takes to earn 1 point, and then how many points you must earn to get any of the perks this club offers. Then compare this to other slot clubs, and find the one which gives you the most. However, do not select your casino for slot play based only on the offers they give from the slot club. You may find that this casino has slots which are set tighter then other casinos whose slot club policies may not be as liberal. In the end, always select your casino based on the availability of the good machines, and then consider the slot club secondarily. When you do everything together, correctly, you will find that by adding the perks you get from your slot play from the slot club, combined with the wins you get on the machines, combined with the losses you *save* by playing the good machine correctly, it will all add up to a nice overall profit in the end. And that's where a large portion of your powerful profits from slots will come from.

What about comps?

"Comp" is a casino slang term for "complimentary." These are the perks you get from slot clubs, as described above. Even if you are not a member of the slot club, immediately after you arrive at that casino, call the operator on the house phone and ask for a slot host. This person is employed by the casino to look after the good players. If you are not yet known at that casino, call the slot host anyway, and introduce yourself. Ask to join the slot club, and the host will help you do that immediately. While you are doing this, ask for the "casino rate." This is a room rate with a substantial discount over the published room rate and is offered to, and reserved for, the casino players. Only slot hosts, casino hosts, and casino executives can get this rate for your room. By asking for the slot host immediately, you are likely to get this rate right away, offered by the host in anticipation of your slot action. If you then play little, you will get the rate this time, but maybe not next time, but the point is you did get it *this* time. If you play a lot and are a good player, then your play will justify that offer, and that will most likely result in your getting other perks, such as the room for free, or an upgrade to a suite, or the total "RF&B," meaning free room, food, and beverage. You will also make a contact at that casino, and the host will give you his or her business card, with a special reservation number available only to casino guests. From that time on, you will be able to call in and usually get a room even if the hotel is "sold out." This is because each hotel keeps a portion of their rooms always reserved for casino guests. If you live near the casino and don't stay at the hotel, then contact the host anyway. You will get to know someone at the casino at a level which can get you a lot of perks and other help, now and in the future. You may be able to get free dinners, buffets, show tickets, special party invitations, and a whole lot of other neat stuff.

What about malfunctions?

It's inevitable. Machines are machines. They break down. The most common breakdown is a coin jam, a ticket jam, or a bill acceptor malfunction. If it happens to you, and it will, then just put the light on and wait for the employee to show up. Most of the time they can fix the problem right then and there, and you can go on playing. On rare occasions, they may have to call a slot mechanic. If this happens, you will wait a little longer. However, if you can't wait, then just tell that to the floorperson, and they will hand-pay you whatever amount of credits you have accumulated, and you can go. They will then shut the machine down, and the slot mechanic will get to it whenever he can. Just don't worry about it if this happens. You didn't break it. Take it easy, relax, have a drink, and wait. Think of the money you are saving by having this relaxing time, waiting. Then, when it's repaired, go on with your play and win.

Slot Strategies

In this chapter, we will talk about two things—a Simple Strategy for Slots, and then The Big Secret. In Chapter 13 there is a Slot Quiz to test your slot playing expertise. Much of what can be described as "slot strategy" actually consists of the principles I described in my Keys to Winning. Those really *are* the best strategy for slots. However, there are some additional hints that can improve your overall profitability potential. It also never hurts to try to simplify the playing process, as well as the strategy information.

The Simple Strategy for Slots is just that—a very simple format, designed to give you the quickest overview of all the information in this book. I don't expect you to remember everything you've read, although it would be best if you did. Meanwhile, here are some quick hints to make your slot play more enjoyable and more profitable. If you want to know a little more, then the Big Secret is for you. I'll show you a method of playing slots that helps me and has helped many players who know how to use it properly. I developed this method and made it available in an abridged format in earlier writings. Here I have upgraded and improved it, and offer it as an addition to your overall slot playing strategies.

Finally, the Slot Quiz in Chapter 13 is designed to be fun and to give you an exercise you can take over and over again. In slot play, there are no hard-and-fast answers. Slot machines, by their very nature, are dependent on many factors and variables. Therefore, trying to quantify it all into identifiable structures is very hard to do. Nevertheless, there are questions which have actual answers, and these answers—if applied correctly—will directly affect your ability to make powerful profits from slots. Slots *can* be played profitably. How well you *do* depends on how much you *know*. The Slot Quiz will provide you with a method of testing this knowledge.

SIMPLE STRATEGY FOR SLOTS

In all that you have just read, and in gambling in general, a few key points apply universally. Even if you remember nothing from this book except these points, you will be way ahead of most other players, and you will, therefore, be a better player.

1. The best way to gauge your *win potential* is:

   Size of bankroll = time at play = more hands played = more chances at the top jackpot (and all pays in between).

2. Whether your bankroll allows you to play quarters, or $1, or $5, or $25 or even $100 slots, this same *win principle* applies:

   Don't shortchange yourself! Play to your win potential based on the size of your bankroll, and *play to win*! This means applying the Keys to Winning, the Selection Principles, and maximum coins at all times.

3. *Set a limit*. Playing to win means you want to take home more money than you brought. Each time you gamble, call it a *session*. Set the amount of money you are prepared to risk for that session. And no more. This is called a *loss limit*. Likewise, set a *win limit*. What if you hit the top jackpot on your machine? Is that enough? It should be. Put it away and play another day.

4. And finally, remember that the advantage you have in gambling is that paying for this form of entertainment does not automatically mean you will spend that money. Unlike any other form of entertainment for which you may pay, gambling allows that you may also win money and be able to go home with more than you brought with you!

These four points apply equally well to all gambling games. For slot machines, however, there is one more important point:

5. *Always play maximum coins*. Whatever the maximum-coin requirement is for the slot machine you have chosen to play, never play without betting the maximum coins allowed for that machine. If you do, you're throwing your money away and enriching the casino.

For example, if your reel slot machine takes 2 coins as a maximum, and it is a $1 denomination machine, the top jackpot may be, say, $1,600 (there are many varieties of jackpots, but this is a good example). On this machine, the top jackpot for 1-coin play may be $400, but it pays $1,600 for the 2-coin play. That's a difference of $1,200! If you play only 1 coin on a machine such as this, and you actually hit the top jackpot, you have just cheated yourself out of an extra pay of $1,200. Instead of having it for yourself, you have given it away to the casino because you did not play the maximum coins and therefore did not force the casino to pay you off at the maximum available pay. If you can't afford to bet the maximum coins, don't play—or don't play at that level. Find a machine on which you can afford to play the maximum coins, or save up and play the machine you want to when you have enough money as your bankroll to play it properly and to your best advantage.

PLAY FOR PROFIT, NOT AS A JOB

Most people don't play slots regularly, every day, like a job. Yes, there are some people who do play slots daily. These are either professional slot players who are making a living from slot machines, slot teams, or, which is more likely, re-tired persons or persons of leisure who simply enjoy the challenge of a good game and the pleasure of great casino service. Most people, however, play slots casually. A few times a year. Perhaps a few times a month, or even a few times a week, depending on how close you are to a casino. Nevertheless, unless you play slots at least five days a week and at least eight hours a day, then you are a casual slot player.

If you play slots on a casual basis, you will be exposed to far greater fluctuations in your fortune than would be the case if you played every day, like a job. A casual player ei-ther will hit any given machine for a sizable profit, or will suffer a loss of the investment, or a portion of that invest-ment. This simply means that on a casual basis, you will either hit the machine at a far greater payoff than its preset withholding percentage indicates, or at far less. Meaning that you will either win a lot more money than you should, percentage-wise, or lose a lot more. Over time, this will smooth out and you will actually be getting, and giving up, something close to the actual hold of that machine, and gaining the profits to which you are entitled by playing in accordance with the advice, and strategies, offered here.

In the short term, however, many of us find that we either experience a nice win very quickly, and then proceed to lose some of it as we continue the enjoyment of our visit to the casino, or we find that we have lost our bring-in investment and have to start hunting for more cash, or consider leaving early. The issue here is to find the best possible combination of skills, machine selection, bankroll, discipline, and other factors that will allow us to exploit the profitability of machine payoffs, while diminishing the inevitable losses.

Some ways of playing slot machines are better than others, but slots are still machines, whose preprogrammed house hold percentage is a constant average. Therefore, if your machine is set to pay back, say, 98 percent, this means that if you play it all the time, 24 hours a day, 7 days a week, and 365 days a year, in the end, on average, you will lose 2 percent of all your money. That's the way it sits.

Of course, this applies to the majority of reel and video reel slots, and not video poker. The reason is that on some video poker machines, skillful perfect play will result in your being able to eke out about 1.1 percent in your favor (for machines which have the programming potential to pay back over 100 percent). Many such machines do exist, but the reality of the small slices of play time for which most players will play them, and the fact that even expert play can often be corrupted by mistakes, unintentional as they may be, means that even these machines are not as good payers as they initially may be touted.

By and large, to be a successful slot player, you will need *at least the majority* of the following attributes:

1. *Enough time at play.* You must be able to remain at play for as long as possible in order to be able to reach closest to the machine's optimum payout potential.

2. *Enough money.* (Commonly referred to as the bankroll.) In order for you to sustain the required play time, depending on the machine you have chosen, you must be able to invest a sufficient amount of money to warrant a successful play period.

3. *Patience.* You must not allow yourself to be distracted or frustrated. Playing slots is not just entertainment, but also a financial decision. Investment begets profits, or losses, depending on how well the investor chooses the investment product. In the case of slot machines, your choices in selection and play, combined with all the Keys to Winning, constitute your "investment analysis" and "profit potential" scenarios. The old adage of "money makes money" applies to slots as well. You can't win anything without first making the investment. How you manage the investment is up to you, and therefore, in slot play, patience, resolve, dedication, and smart application of your investment goals are necessary for relatively steady success.

4. *Knowing when to quit.* No slot machine will continually pay out. They will "take" and "give," usually in cycles. Sometimes a machine will shower you with coins, while at other times you may get one of the better-paying machines but one which is in the "take" cycle. To know when to quit is to protect your investment. That's where strategy comes into play. (See "The Big Secret," which follows.)

5. *When is enough enough?* Well, that's a toss-up. It depends on what the value of the money happens to be for you. Generally, I'd say that any win over and above

your initial starting investment is profit, and therefore something you should pocket and keep.

6. *How often to play?* That depends on your available time. Generally, I'd say about once a month, and in dedicated periods for profitable play. But that depends, to a large extent, on your time, access to a casino, and available capital.

7. *How long to play?* On a $1 machine that takes 2 coins as maximum, about two hours should be enough to run the machine through its paces. However, you should monitor your pay and adapt your playing time according to the relevant requirements listed earlier. For $1 machines that take 3 coins as maximum, this time period will be determined by your bankroll. So is the case for $5 machines and higher.

8. *Which casino to play in?* Here's where your personal investigation comes into good effect. Whichever casinos are in your immediate area, call them first, ask for Public Relations, and have them describe to you the kinds of slots they have, and how many they have. Usually the more slots a casino has, the better the overall choices. However, some smaller, or start-up, casinos may also be a good bet for your slot play, because they may have better-paying machines in order to attract customers. An excellent method for reviewing casinos is to take a really close look at the advertisements they place in gaming magazines, periodicals, newspapers, or through direct mail to slot club members. Most of the kind of information you'll want appears in these advertisements, periodicals, or flyers, so take advantage of this free information and look, read, and understand. Then call, if you want to know more before you go there. If you can't get any decent information from the PR Department, try the

Marketing Department, or the Player's Club, or even ask for a slot host or casino host.

9. *Which kind of slot machine?* As a rule of thumb when playing reel slots, don't play "gimmicky" machines, the kinds that blink and buzz and so on with various "bonus" or "mystery" features. They are entertaining, but not necessarily a good investment. Video slots are different. On video slots, many of the various bonus pays are actually part of the game's beneficial pay program, and therefore your decisions should be modified to reflect the differences between reel slots and video slots. All of the advice shown here applies to both, but the video slots are far more complicated and will require more of your dedicated time to learn what the most important play and pay features are.

If you play in this manner you will have a better, more consistent shot at profitable play. Of course, you might be one of those very lucky players who will always win, in which case bless you. For the rest of us, I'd stick to the above—and, yes, a little bit of luck every now and then goes a long way.

THE BIG SECRET

The above Simple Strategy for Slots, and the hints above, are very basic. They are designed only for a quick overview. Although they are very useful for players who don't wish to learn a whole lot, for those of you who want to do a little more, here is a method which I have successfully used myself, and which has been a time-proven way of playing slots for consistent profits. You should remember, however, that no one wins all the time. Even these methods will not always works. Nevertheless, when you view all your sessions as a *combination of events*, rather than focus on just one event at a time, as most people do, you will realize that your sessions combined produce an end-result win. As I mentioned in my book *Powerful Profits from Blackjack*, you can win only about 41 percent of the time, yet still wind up with a *financial profit* at the end. How well you do will depend on how well you can apply the methods and strategies described in this book.

Skills in slots are highly dependent on the abilities of the player. This is also the case with blackjack, and indeed with all gambling in general. Two players playing the same machine in the same manner may have directly opposite experiences and results. For these reasons, and others already mentioned, you must always remember that whatever results you achieve from your slot play are not to be viewed as isolated, individual events. They are all part of a protracted series of events. These events cumulatively will provide you with the proper and correct results in the end. How many of these events you will have depends, again, on you. The more of these events you have, the better the odds of your profitability, if you play correctly. The fewer the events, the greater likelihood that your events may not result in the kind of profits which a protracted series will make possible.

Regardless of how you view this, the fact remains that any series of events can be as short as 2, or as long as you can make it. In the case of 2 events only, your results cannot be expected to reflect any methodology, no matter how scientific, or how accurate. Two events simply aren't enough. How many events are enough? Again, it depends. I would say that 10 events in a session are enough, and that 10 sessions should be performed before any results are tabulated. This will give you 100 events. If you allocate $100 to each event, over 1 session, this will come to $1,000. Over 10 sessions, this will come to $10,000. Don't be too concerned if the thought of a $10,000 bankroll seems far out of your reach. You can adapt these figures to your own budget by looking at the bankroll guidelines in "Keys to Winning." Also, remember that the $10,000 is a *cumulative* figure over *all* these sessions. So what you actually need to start is only that first $1,000. This you divide into 10 events, each for $100. If you play $1 two-coin reel slots, this will give you more than enough of an opportunity—cumulatively over all sessions—to drive the profits home.

It would be best, of course, if you had that $10,000 as your total bankroll, not necessarily in your pocket or purse, but handy, should you need it. The amount you should actually have with you for this method is about $3,000. As each session continues, and each event occurs, the amounts which you have available will fluctuate. In the end, when you have completed the process, you should have a profit. If you don't, then you did something wrong. Perhaps you played something else with that money, and didn't account for this. That's a no-no. You *cannot* use this particular bankroll for anything else. Just these sessions, with this method, and that's it. If you want to do anything else, then you need additional funds. For example, if you need to buy dinner, show tickets, souvenirs, pay for your hotel room, or anything like that, none of this can come from your slot playing bankroll dedicated to these sessions, under this methodology. If you take any amount away from it, chances are you will forget you did that, and so at the end of your session string you may not show a profit, or not as much profit as you should have. If this is so, then you should examine your *uses* of that *bankroll*, rather than the method. If there is still a loss, then something happened during the string of sessions. Keep an accurate record of everything, so you can go back to it later and re-examine what you did, when, how, and why, and what was the result. In this way, you will always know where you stand and what happened. Make notes. Keep an accounting ledger. It's not hard. The best side benefit will be that you will have an accurate record for the IRS, and when it comes time to pay your taxes, you will have the proper format by which you can itemize and deduct all your losses, leaving only your profits as income.

Now, to The Big Secret. This is based on the above mentioned methodology, with 10 events per session at $100 per event, with 10 sessions in a block, for a total stake of $1,000 per session, equals $10,000 per session block. Your total bring-in bankroll should be $3,000, with your total playing bankroll available at $10,000. Here's how this method will work:

1. If you have DOUBLED your starting event bankroll, *quit* and end this event.
2. If you have MORE than 75 percent OVER AND ABOVE your starting bankroll, but LESS than 100 percent profit, *quit* this event.
3. If you have LESS than 75 percent over and above your starting bankroll, but MORE than 50 percent over your starting event amount, *cash out* and play that *same* machine again—as Event #2—following the principles from Rule #1, and so on.
4. If you have LESS than 50 percent over and above your starting event bankroll, *quit* and start a *new* event on *another* machine.
5. If you have exactly the SAME amount as your event bankroll—even money—*quit* this event and start a *new* event on *another* machine.
6. If at the end of ANY event you have LESS than your starting event stake, *quit* and start a *new* event on *another* machine.

There you have it. This method—applicable to the traditional reel spinners—is a very workable method of play. It produces profits regularly, after the series of events and sessions has been tabulated cumulatively, all other factors being taken into account. At the very least, this method will *limit your losses*, because *it forces you to quit every time you have less than the amount you started with at the beginning of each event.* For that reason alone, this is a worthwhile method of playing reel slots.

The Slot Quiz:
Know Your Slot Machine

I have now told you just about everything that can be shared about slot machines. If you have been reading carefully, and understood what I was trying to let you know, or if perhaps you think you may already know most of the information required to be a winner, here's your chance to test your skills!

It's time for the Slot Quiz!

Here is a list of multiple-choice questions to which a successful slot player should know the correct answers. Score 5 points for each correct answer and deduct 5 points for each wrong answer. At the end of this chapter you can find out how good your slot player's knowledge really is. This is the final exam for Slots 101.

All of these questions have a *direct impact* on how well you will do when playing slot machines. A high score can significantly improve your chances at consistent slot wins. So take out your pen or pencil and get ready.

1. The best kind of *reel* slot machine is:
   A. One that looks very interesting.
   B. One that offers double-pay symbols which also substitute for all other symbols.
   C. One that has really nice-looking symbols on it.
   D. One offering double-pay symbols that are wild.

2. The best "bonus" *reel* slot machine is:
   A. One that has double symbols which are wild, or has double symbols which substitute for all other symbols, and pays scatters.
   B. One that has triple pay symbols or 5-times pay symbols or 10-times pay symbols.
   C. One that has multi-pay symbols that are wild and substitute for all other symbols and pay scatters.
   D. One that has all of the above.

3. It is better to play machines which:
   A. Are advertised as "Up to 98 percent payback."
   B. Are advertised as "94.7 percent payback."
   C. Are not advertised or promoted at all.
   D. Look like they pay a lot.

4. A "double-up" *reel* slot machine is:
   A. One that takes two coins to play.
   B. One that takes twice as much money to play.
   C. One that pays twice as much as another.
   D. One that has "double bonus" pay symbols.

5. When playing a *reel* slot machine, it is better to play one that:
   A. Has more than three reels.
   B. Has multiple reels and paylines.
   C. Has three reels.
   D. Has four reels.

6. It is best to play a *reel* slot machine that is:
   A. A 25¢ per coin machine.
   B. A $1 per coin machine or $5 per coin machine.

C. A 5¢ per coin machine.

D. All of the above.

7. When playing any slot machine, it is better to:
   A. Sometimes bet 1 coin and sometimes bet maximum coins.
   B. Often bet less than maximum coins.
   C. Always play maximum coins.
   D. Bet different amounts per spin and vary the betting.

8. The reels on *reel* slot machines are controlled:
   A. Mechanically by the use of stoppers.
   B. By the use of lead weights.
   C. By computer chips.
   D. By the luck of the draw.

9. The winning or losing combinations are determined:
   A. By luck.
   B. Randomly whenever the reels stop.
   C. As soon as the first coin, or credit, is played.
   D. By the symbols on the reels.

10. All modern slot machines, reel or video, are:
    A. Controlled by a computer and a computer chip.
    B. Controlled by what is known as a Random Number Generator (RNG).
    C. Controlled by changing the payoff program.
    D. All of the above.

11. Video slots are:
    A. Better than reel slots.
    B. Worse than reel slots.
    C. Too complicated.
    D. Too hard to hit because of all the combinations and paylines.

12. When playing 45 nickels at a time, it is better to:
    A. Keep at it until you win big.
    B. Better to play this many nickels than less.
    C. Go play a $1 machine with 2 coins as maximum bet instead.
    D. Go play a 25¢ machine instead.

13. Playing nickel machines is:
    A. Better than other kinds because it doesn't cost as much to play.
    B. Better because you can bet up to 25 coins and 45 coins per bet on some machines.
    C. Better not to play nickel machines at all.
    D. Better because you can play longer.

14. The best *average* bankroll for 25¢ *reel* slots is:
    A. $50.
    B. $200.
    C. $350.
    D. $600.

15. The best bankroll for a $1 machine is:
    A. $300.
    B. $400.
    C. $600.
    D. $1,000 or more.

16. *Reel* slot machines are better than video slot machines:
    A. Because they pay better.
    B. Because they are simpler to play.
    C. Because there aren't as many combinations to worry about.
    D. No better or worse because they are in reality both computers.

17. When a slot machine is listed as paying back 99 percent, that means:
    A. The machine may pay this much when you play.
    B. It will pay out this much over the fiscal year life cycle.
    C. It will pay out 99¢ for every dollar you play.
    D. It will pay out that much on average each 50,000 spins.

18. A "jackpot" is:
    A. The top amount you can win.
    B. Anything which requires a hand-pay from the attendant.
    C. Anything which is more than you invested.
    D. Any of the top three amounts listed on the payoff display.

19. A "progressive" slot machine is:
    A. Better to play than non-progressives because you can win so much more.
    B. Better to play than non-progressives because there are more pays.
    C. Not as good as other kinds of slot machines which take that many coins.
    D. Worth only a trial investment because the odds of winning the jackpot are too high.

20. When playing a "progressive" slot machine, you should:
    A. Only bet maximum coins when you feel like it will hit.
    B. Sometimes play less than maximum coins to save your bankroll and play longer.
    C. Always play maximum coins no matter what.
    D. First see how other people play and then adapt what they do.

21. It is better to play a *reel* slot machine which:
    A. Takes 3 coins as maximum.
    B. Takes 2 coins as maximum.
    C. Takes more than 3 coins as maximum.
    D. Takes bills as well as coins.

22. Video slot machines are:
    A. Better to play because of the multiple lines and betting amounts you can play.
    B. Not as good as regular slots because they are only video screens.
    C. Worse than any other kind of slots because you can't tell what wins.
    D. Worse than any other kinds of slots because they cost so much to play.

23. If you're playing a video slot machine which has up to 9 paylines, you should:
    A. Only play 1 line.
    B. Only play 3 lines.
    C. Only play 5 lines.
    D. Always play all lines.

24. If you're playing a video slot machine which has up to 9 paylines and allows you to bet from 1 coin per line (9-coin bet) up to 5 coins per line (45-coin bet) you should:
    A. Never bet the full amount of 45 coins per bet because it's so expensive.
    B. Sometimes bet the full 45 coins and see how the machine is playing.
    C. Only bet no more than 25 coins per bet.
    D. Always bet the maximum coins no matter what the total coin-per-bet amount is.

25. The best slot machine game to play, relative to cost of investment, is:
    A. Reel slot machines.
    B. Video slot machines.
    C. Video poker.
    D. Video keno.

Well, that's the end of the questions. Here are the answers, and reasons for them:

1. The answer is B. Machines which have symbols which double all pays *and* also substitute for *all other symbols* are the most liberal reel slots you can find. There aren't many of them on the casino floor, but they can be found. They are better than any of the other machines, because these other kinds are infrequent payers, and although the jackpots may be terrific, your investment and play time relative to win expectancy is better on the "double-up" machines, overall, for the short-term slice of your action while playing.

2. The answer is B. Whatever kind of slot machine it is, if it has multi-pay symbols which are wild *and* substitute for all other symbols *and* pay scatters, then you have a machine which will traditionally pay 98 percent or better as payback. This is the kind you want, but you will have to look for it. Read the payoff display and pay combinations carefully. Even a machine which has at least two of these features will be among the best.

3. The answer is B. Machines which are advertised as "up to . . .", do not *all* have to pay out that amount. If it says "up to," then this means that *some* of the machines pay more than that, but *many others pay less*, with the *average* over all the machines so advertised being that percentage. However, machines listed as "Payback of 94.7 percent" or

any such payback which does *not* have the words "up to" in front of it means that *all* these machines pay that amount, and not just the average between many of their kind.

4. The answer is D.

5. The answer is C.

6. The answer is B. The most liberal slots are usually $1 and $5 machines. Machines which take higher coins, such as $25 coins, or even $100 coins or more, do not necessarily have the better pay programs. Casinos know that many more people will play the $5 slots than $100 slots, and more still will play $1 slots, so they make these paybacks better. Even at only a 2 percent house edge, the casinos still make millions of dollars in profit because of the volume of players playing these machines. But this is also good for you, because you can get a better-paying machine for your gaming investment.

7. The answer is C. Never play any slot machine without the maximum-coin bet. If you do, you are giving the casino more profits even if you win, because you are not forcing them to pay you the full amount of your win by not playing the maximum coins. Don't listen to anyone who says differently, because such proponents don't know a hog from a horse's rear end.

8. The answer is C. All modern slot machines are controlled by computer chips, regardless of what they appear to be. There is absolutely no difference between a slot machine that has reels which look like they are mechanical and a video reel slot machine. The programs which run them, and the computer chips which control them, are all the same (with different game payout programs for different kinds of machines, but that's not the subject of this question).

9. The answer is C. As soon as the first coin trips (clocks) the machine's sensors, or the first credit is played, the end-

result combinations of that spin or pull are already determined. The fact that it takes a few seconds for the reels to
stop is just window-dressing. The machines have a program
which runs millions of possible combinations per microsecond, and the instant the coin trips the sensor, or the credit
does so, this process stops and decides the outcome of that
spin. And yes, playing maximum coins is still the best way
to play because that allows you to cash in on the payoffs
closest to the true odds of the machine's payoff program,
especially on the "buy-a-pay" machines.

10. The answer is D. All modern slot machines are controlled by a computer, which has what is commonly referred to as the RNG, a program which controls the
randomness of the combinations. All slots are controlled by
changing the payoff programs to whatever the casino wants
it to be, usually by means of changing the game's programming chip (which has to be done in accordance with gaming
regulations and must be reported and supervised and veri-
fied, so no "cheating" is possible).

11. The answer is A. Video slots are much better to play
than any other kind of slots, because of the tremendous pays
which can be achieved by the use of multiple paylines and
multiple coins-per-bet. The fact that you can bet 45
coins—or more—per spin means that you will be getting
much better overall payouts than on any other kind of machine, when you hit.

12. The answer is C. Playing 45 nickels per bet is in reality $2.25 per bet. Yet the actual winnings you can achieve
are far lower than this amount of action should give you.
You will be far better off to play a $1 machine with a 2-coin
maximum. You'll get bigger and better pays and still save
25¢ per pull. Video slots which take this many coins are
best played at the 25-cent per-line level, or even $1 if you

can find them. This is high action, but the payoffs are worth it, and are better, overall, than the equivalent action on $10 or higher reel slots.

I also wish to point out that this answer is not in conflict with the answer in question 11. While the video slots are a good bet precisely because of your ability to wager more coins per line, and because they have the availability of multiple lines and many such derived additional payouts and wins and bonuses, the financial fact remains that as matters apply *specifically to this question* (question 12), your $2.25 wager on the nickel video reel slots can be better spent on a $2 two-coin reel slot machine. The differences are in the *kind* of machine you are going to play. For example, if your video reel slot machine allows you to wager 90 coins or more, has 20 lines or more, or has other features such as we have discussed, then there is a par-equivalency between these answers to questions 11 and 12. In that case, both answers would be equal. The same applies for the video slots which are in the 25¢-per-credit denomination. Although this will now cost you $11.25 per pull (at 45 coins per bet), the payoffs even on the most rudimentary hits will be in the hundreds, and even thousands, of dollars. This will then make this machine a better bet than the $1 reel slots, as suggested by the answer to question 12. However, at this point you should also consider going to the $5 reel slots, and wagering two coins for a total wager of $10, and find out if this may be the game more suited to your taste. Ultimately, these answers here *are limited to the very specific games to which they refer.* You will have to be able to judge for yourself which games and machines are better suited to your play, based on your analysis of the *kind* of machine you are about to play.

13. The answer is C. Most of the time you will spend more than you can win—even if you do hit the jackpot. Al-

though there are several video reel slots, which offer very good value for your investment, if all you have is a choice of nickel machines you will be better off to go and play 25¢ or higher multi-line machines instead, or $1 or $5 reel slots with 2 coins max (as discussed above).

14. The answer is D. You can get a lot of play for $600. If you are playing at 3 coins per pull (75¢), your $600 bankroll will last you for 800 pulls—without hitting any pays. And that's a lot of pulls to get some good pays and have a good shot at the jackpot. Refer also to the chapter that introduces the Keys to Winning, and modify your personal bankroll accordingly, if your playing preferences so dictate.

15. The answer is D. On a $1 slot machine you will need at least a minimum of $1,000 to give it a good tryout. On a 2-coin maximum machine this will only be 500 pulls without a payoff, and you'll traditionally need twice that many pulls to tackle the machine's fickle cycles. Less than that amount, and you're not playing to win—you're then playing only for entertainment, and thus enriching the casino. In fact, you should have at least $3,000 for such play to provide you with the best shot at the top jackpots. Refer also to the chapter on Keys to Winning, and modify your personal bankroll accordingly, if your playing preferences so dictate.

16. The answer is D. There is no inherent difference between reel slot machines and video slot machines (other than the payoff programs, but that isn't the subject of this question). In fact, reel slot machines *are* video slot machines, and their programming principles are the same as any other video slot machine. Just because you see "reels" in the window makes no difference. You could be seeing anything else, and it would still be the same. It's the chip inside which holds the machine's game. The rest is just the box and the display.

17. The answer is B. The payoff percentages listed are *averages* over a year-long cycle based on millions of pulls. Such a machine will, in the end, pay out this much on all pays and hand-pays combined. It will *never* pay out 99¢ for each coin played, nor will it pay you $99 out of each $100 for that particular session. It may pay more, or less, when you happen to be sitting there playing it, but overall in the end all such pays will equal 99 percent of all the money played through the machine, or as close as is statistically feasible and acceptable. And so on for any machine which is listed as paying back a specified *flat* percentage.

18. The answer is C. If you have made a profit, *any* kind of profit, you are way ahead of the reality of the machine's preprogrammed house edge. Therefore, it is a jackpot, even if it is only $1, or even less. Whatever the amount is that you have made *over and above your initial investment*, this is a jackpot, and means you have defeated the house edge by a huge percentage differential!

19. The answer is both C and D. Progressives do not pay well, and that is so because some of the money goes to build the giant progressive top award (the generally accepted estimate is from about 5 percent to 10 percent of all the money put through the machines which are part of such a progressive link). These machines are good to play occasionally, for a "trial" investment, but you are far better off playing other kinds of slots which take the same number of coins as maximum. (Score +5 points if you picked *either* C or D.)

20. The answer is C. If that isn't obvious, you'll need to go back to school for some extra lessons in arithmetic. You *can't win the giant award on any progressive machine if you do not play the maximum coins*! Period!

21. The answer is B. Remember, here the question has to do with *reel* slot machines, and *not* video slots. On a reel

slot machine, 2-coin maximum is the best play overall, as long as this kind of machine is one which *only* takes 2 coins as maximum. If it takes more than 2 coins, you should still always play the maximum coins, but that isn't *this* question.

22. The answer is A. Video slots are so much better than any other kind of slot machine precisely because they allow for so many paylines, pay options, and higher maximum-coin limits (understanding that we have learned to *select* the correct machines, and learn what they do and how they pay, and thus be able to apply our skills and knowledge; however, that was not *this* question, so be aware of it before you start thinking this answer is in conflict with the other answers).

23. The answer is D.

24. The answer is D.

25. The answer is D. As curious as this may sound to some, video keno offers the best payouts *relative to cost of investment* of any kind of slot machine. And yes, it is a slot machine. For a 25¢ bet, you can win over $5,000 on some combinations, and that's a huge payoff potential relative to the base investment. Therefore—and *only* for video keno—I advise that the general "always play maximum coins per bet" be modified. *Only for video keno!!* On this game, and this game only, you can bet less than maximum coins and still get a very high payoff relative to the amount invested.

Scoring

Give yourself 5 points for each correct answer, and take away 5 points for each wrong answer. Score your totals as follows:

100–125 total points: you are a professional! You should form a slot syndicate and play all the time. This means you are the Professor of Slots, and congratulations!!

75–95 total points: You are very good! But you could use a little more study.

50–70 total points: You need some help, but you're pretty good.

25–45 total points: You're obviously playing just for entertainment and aren't particularly concerned with winning. Perhaps you should try something different, like fishing.

Below 25 total points: Casinos LOVE YOU !! They will invite you back over and over again, because they know they'll get all your money all the time. Save yourself the trip, and just mail it in. Or better still, mail it to me. I'll play it for you, and when I win I'll send you back a 10 percent profit. Better than any stock market, right?

And that's the end of this quiz.

Postscript

I have tried to do as much as possible within the confines of this book. Most people think slot machines are the easiest and simplest forms of gambling. I hope I have convinced you that this is far from the truth. Actually, slot machines are among the most complex gambling devices and games now available. More and more complex machines and games are being developed even as you are reading this. By the time you finish reading this paragraph, at least ten new slot machines will be installed in casinos in the U.S.A., with about one hundred new games—or more—being developed at any one time.

Slot machines exist for one purpose, and one purpose only: to make money for their owners. In order to accomplish this, the owners must provide you, the players, with machines and games that you will *want* to play. These must be entertaining, easy to play and understand, and *must offer good pays*! If a machine wasn't all that interesting, and wasn't all that entertaining, but it paid really, really well, then everyone would flock to that machine, and it would be the most wildly successful slot machine ever made. That's why the owners of slots always insist not only that their machines be interesting and entertaining, but that they also *pay*. After all, if these slot machines did not pay, then players would soon find that out and would refuse to play them. Why would you want to play a machine that didn't pay you back? You wouldn't, of course. That's why it is a misconception that casinos, slot machine owners, operators, and manufacturers only want machines that will make money for *them* and take it *from* you. While it is true that slot machines exist only for the one reason stated above, the other side of this coin is equally important. If the players of these machines would not play them, then these machines would not exist. Ergo, the owners would not make any money from owning the slots.

What is often missed in discussions of slot machines is the question of *why they are played*. The answers often given are: The game is fun; The machine is entertaining; The game is based on a popular theme; The look, feel, colors, etc., are attractive; and so on, and on, in marketing research jargon. These may be valid inferences—up to a point. Actually, the real answers to why the machines are played often have little to do with the machine, or game itself. Many times it has a lot more to do with the way in which the machine is packaged, as well as the actual playing conditions on the casino floor. As well as the game may perform in the laboratory, or in market testing and focus groups, or whatever the field trials may be, when it is finally released to the general public, the game can suffer from several problems that may have gone completely undetected throughout this entire process.

For example, the machine may be annoying to the players. It may make silly sounds which are too noisy, too tinny, too frequent, or too childish. The cabinetry may be badly designed, causing players to have to reach into narrow coin trays or coin chutes, or the machine is too tall, too slanted, it has padding in front of it which spills drinks and traps dirt, or it has a screen which is mounted on an angle which reflects the casino lighting, thereby causing players eye fatigue, and so on and on and on. I have heard thousands of such points from hundreds of thousands of slot players I have interviewed over a decade, and they all say almost the same things. Yet all the machines still have most of the same problems. Perhaps eventually the manufacturers will ask me, and I will be able to tell them the actual, real-world truth.

As far as the players are concerned, however, the main point is whether the machine will actually pay. Not just "phantom" pays, which are more "teasers" than anything of actual value, but real, dollar-making, take-home-money-making pays. Value for the patronage. Value for the play. That's what will determine the machine's success, in the final player's tally.

In this book, I have tried to teach you how to find the good machines, how to recognize the differences among them, and how to approach playing them with the best chance of success. Powerful profits from slots are possible. What I have written was selected precisely to offer you this edge. How well you do with it—well, dear friend, that will have to be up to you.

Acknowledgments

First and foremost, I wish to thank my dear mother, Georgina S. Royer, for her lifetime of help, guidance, and assistance. She is a remarkable lady who fully deserves notice for her tremendous abilities and her steadfast faith in me.

I also wish to thank my literary agents, Greg Dinkin and Frank Scatoni. Greg is an accomplished author in his own right, and Frank a widely respected book editor. Through their Agency, Venture Literary, they recognized the value of what I had to offer as an author of books on casino games and gaming. Without their efforts, this book and the others in this series, would never have come to exist.

My thanks also to Bruce Bender, at Kensington Publishing Corp., who publishes this series. He recognized that this book, and the others in this series, offers valuable insight into the casino games as they really are, and that this book will enable almost all players to realize a happy and profitable casino experience. I thank Bruce and the staff of Kensington for their help in this process, and in particular that wonderful lady, Ann LaFarge, my editor.

I extend my gratitude and thanks to my longtime friend Tom Caldwell for the many things he has done to help me and enrich my life. I also send my thanks to Norreta, Sean, and Brent, for reasons they all know.

To all my other friends and associates in the gaming business, from owners, managers, and senior executives to hosts and supervisors, you all know who you are, and I thank you.

I thank my friends in Australia, Neil and his family, Lilli and little MRM (Mark), Ormond College, University of Melbourne, the Governor of Victoria and my former Master, Sir Davis McCaughey. Also his Proctorial Eminence R. A. Dwyer, Esq. (I still have the Swiss knife you gave me more than twenty years ago), and the Alumni Association of the University of Wollongong, NSW, department of Philosophy, and Professor Chipman.

My grateful appreciation I also extend to Mr. Laurence E. Levit, C.P.A., of Los Angeles, who has been my steadfast friend, accountant, and adviser for two decades, and whose faith in me and my work has never faltered. A truer friend a man rarely finds. Also to Mr. Michael Harrison, attorney at law in Beverly Hills, California, whose expertise and help have made my life more secure.

At this time, I wish to single out, in particular, Mr. Ed Rogich from IGT. I wish to thank him for his foresight and his much appreciated assistance during the process of writing this book. I also wish to thank my longtime friend Mr. Rick Sorensen, also from IGT, for all his help. Both Mr. Rogich and Mr. Sorensen were directly instrumental in providing me with the kind of information I needed. Without their assistance, I would not have been able to show you the photographs of those many machines and games I like so much. I also wish to thank Mr. Joe Kaminkow for his support, as well as Connie Fox, Dawn Cox, Todd Brown, Cynthia White, and Harold Shotwell. Without the support of all these people, and their valuable help and assistance, it would have been very much more difficult to tell you about the slots I wanted to write about, and which I have played, and which I wanted to showcase in this book. My thanks also to all the staff, executives, and officers, of International Game Technology (IGT), of Reno, Nevada. You are tops with me!

Finally, to all those whose paths have crossed mine, and who have for one reason or another stopped awhile and visited: I may no longer remember your names, but I do remember what it meant to have those moments.

Thank you!

Copyrights and Trademarks

Throughout this book, I have mentioned slot machines that are products, either owned by, or often based upon registered, copyright, and trademark ownership, of either IGT or third parties. All are used herein by permission. The following information acknowledges such ownership of these products, images, logos, and other distinctive features as indicated.

IGT® AND THIRD-PARTY TRADEMARK LISTS

The following are registered, copyright, and/or trademarked by International Game Technology (IGT), of Reno, Nevada, used by permission:

12 Times Pay™; Black Rhino®; Cleopatra®; Diamond Cinema™; Diamond Mine™; Dollars Deluxe®; Double Bucks®—Design also—® on design; Double Diamond®; Double Diamond 2000®; Double Diamond Deluxe®; Double Diamond Mine®; Double Diamond Run™; Double Dollars®; Double Pay™; Double Red, White & Blue™; Double Ten Times Pay™; Five Times Pay™; Five Times Pay (Black & White)™; Game King®; Game King Plus™; IGT®; IGT Gaming Systems™; IGT University™; IGT University®; IGT.com®; IGT's Guide to Video Gaming™; Integrated Voucher System™; International Game Technology®; Little Green Men®—Design also—® on design; Little Green Men, Jr.™; Lucky Deal Poker®; Market Madness™; Megabucks®; MegaJackpots™; MegaJackpots Instant Winners™—Design also—™ on design; Midnight Madness™; Money Storm®; Multi-Denomination®; Multi-Line Madness™; My Rich Uncle™; Nickelmania®; Nickels Deluxe®; Quartermania®; Quarters Deluxe®; Red, White & Blue®; Regis'

Cash Club™; Slotto™; Super 8 Race®; Super Cherry™; Super Double Pays®; Ten Times Pay®; Texas Tea®; Top Dollar Deluxe®; Touchscreen™; Triple Bucks™; Triple Cash™; Triple Diamond®; Triple Diamond Deluxe®; Triple Dollars®; Triple Double Diamond™; Triple Double Red, White & Blue™; Triple Jackpot®— Design also—® on design; Triple Lucky 7's™; Vision Series®; Wheel of Gold™; Wild Cherry®; Wild Cherry Pie®; Wild Diamonds®; Wild Five Times Pay™; Wild Star®; Wild Thing!™

THIRD-PARTY TRADEMARK LISTS

The following are registered, copyright, and/or trademarked by International Game Technology (IGT), of Reno, Nevada, and/or by third parties under appropriate arrangements between IGT and such third parties, and are used by permission:

$1,000,000 Pyramid™ "$1,000,000 Pyramid"™ & © 2002 CPT Holdings, Inc. All Rights Reserved.

The Addams Family™—"The Addams Family" Developed under agreement with Monaco Entertainment Corporation. "Uncle Fester" image™/© 2002 The Estate of Jackie Coogan licensed by Global Icons, Los Angeles, CA 90034. All Rights Reserved. Mark requires ™.

Austin Powers™—"Austin Powers"™ New Line Productions, Inc. © 2002 New Line Productions, Inc. All Rights Reserved. Mark requires ™.

Elvira®—"Elvira" and "Mistress of the Dark" are trademarks of Queen "B" Productions. Rights used by permission. "Elvira's Haunted Hills" is the copyright and trademark of Elvira Movie Company, LLC. Rights used by permission.

Evel Knievel™—"Evel Knievel" © 2002 Robert Craig Knievel aka Evel Knievel. Mark requires ™.

Harley-Davidson® "Harley-Davidson" © 2002 H-D.All Rights Reserved. Mark requires ®.

Humphrey Bogart™—"Humphrey Bogart"™/© 2001 Bogart, Inc. licensed by CMG Worldwide CMGWW.com Mark requires ™.

I Dream of Jeannie™—"I Dream of Jeannie"™ & © 2002 CPT Holdings, Inc. All Rights Reserved. Mark requires ™.

I Love Lucy®—"I LOVE LUCY" is a registered trademark of CBS Worldwide, Inc. Images of Lucille Ball and Desi Arnaz are licensed by Desilu, too, LLC. Licensing by Unforgettable Licensing. Mark requires ®.

Ingrid Bergman™ "Ingrid Bergman"™/© 2001 Estate of Ingrid Bergman licensed by CMG Worldwide CMGWW.com. Mark requires ™.

Marilyn Monroe™ "Marilyn Monroe"™/© Marilyn Monroe, LLC, licensed by CMG Worldwide MarilynMonroe.com. Mark requires ™.

The Munsters™—The Munsters is a copyright of Kayro-Vue Productions and a trademark of Universal Studios. Licensed by Universal Studios Licensing LLLP. All Rights Reserved. By arrangement with Universal Television, a division of Universal City Studios, Inc. Developed under agreement with Monaco Entertainment Corporation. Designed under agreement with Game Refuge, Inc. and Great Circle Gaming Corporation. Mark requires ™.

Richard Petty Driving Experience™. Mark requires ™.

Sinatra™—The "Sinatra™" game is an IGT product manufactured in association with Sheffield Enterprises, Inc. and Bristol Productions Limited Partnership. Mark requires ™.

Slingo®—SLINGO® is a registered trademark of Slingo, Inc. Mark requires ®.

Wheel of Fortune®—"Wheel of Fortune" is a registered trademark of Califon Productions, Inc. "Wheel of Fortune" © 2002 Califon Productions, Inc. All Rights Reserved. Mark requires ®.

Index